Dan Hare

REGRETS,
THEY'VE HAD A FEW

PRACTICAL WISDOM FROM THE AGED

www.trafford.com

North America & International
toll-free: 1 888 232 4444 (USA & Canada)
phone: 250 383 6864 ♦ fax: 250 383 6804
email: info@trafford.com

The United Kingdom & Europe
phone: +44 (0)1865 487 395 ♦ local rate: 0845 230 9601
facsimile: +44 (0)1865 481 507 ♦ email: info.uk@trafford.com

10 9 8 7 6

TABLE OF CONTENTS

ACKNOWLEDGMENTS

THIS BOOK would never have been completed without the help of several dedicated people. After surviving the cost and time of many years of schooling, my wife, Lynette, was again patient as I left home hundreds of times to arrange and carry out interviews over a two and a half year period. When I returned she would enter all the information on the computer from my hand written and barely legible interview sheets. My friend Sheila Isaacs helped me more than she knows, especially in the last stretch. It was with her help that I was able to secure the interviews I needed to finish the project without being overcome by discouragement. She vouched for me and actively arranged interviews, and for that I am eternally grateful. Many thanks go to the care home directors and workers who allowed me access to those in their care and helped me make the connections I needed. Thanks to Kimberly Baskerville for assistance with photos, layout and website. A special thanks to all the wonderful people who agreed to be interviewed and had a tremendous impact on my life.

CHAPTER 1

THE PEOPLE AND THE PROCESS

HAVE YOU EVER WATCHED old people and wondered about them, their struggles, their heartaches, their triumphs? Have you imagined them as young people and wondered what they were like, handsome or beautiful, embracing life? What did they do for work, how many children did they have, and were they happily married? Did they have a happy life, or was their life full of heartache and regret? And have you ever wondered how people who have endured so many years see the world now and their place in it? I wrote this book to satisfy my curiosity and pass on what they said.

I have spent much of my adult life attending college, university, and seminary. During those years I learned a lot, but because I am very practical minded I always evaluate whatever I learn by how it enhances my understanding of the world and my place in it.

Professors make a career of having students read many things that they will forget once the test is over. Since I never considered myself an academic, in the true sense, I looked for simpler insights that resonated with me and then made them part of my personal understanding. It has been my experience that the best lessons in life are the simplest ones. In university I read the books and wrote the tests but I was really looking to gather gems of wisdom. So instead of becoming a scholar I became a gem hunter gathering practical pearls of wisdom wherever I could find them. And there were many.

When my days of formal education ended it occurred to me that because every person has to make some sense of the world, whatever their circumstance, there must be many people who will never teach a university course but also have gems of wisdom to share based on their life experience. So in order to find some of these gems I designed an interview with questions about virtually every aspect of life and met with over three hundred people who had reached the golden age of sixty-five and beyond to see what practical life lessons could be drawn from their wisdom and experience.

My simple reasoning was that people who have reached an advanced age have endured a great deal and had many years to assess the world and find their place in it. So began the journey that was the inspiration for this book. In retrospect, my expectations were exceeded and I met some wonderful people who enriched my life by sharing some of the practical wisdom I was looking for. This is a gold mine.

This is not a scientific survey but thoughts from a random collection of people. The only criterion for an interview was that people were over the age of sixty-five. If they were willing, I interviewed people anywhere and everywhere I could meet them. I arranged interviews and visited people in their homes, apartments, care homes, hospitals and even a couple in public places like restaurants.

Over a period of more than two years I interviewed many people who were well advanced in years, the oldest being one hundred, and many who were ill, some terminally. There are many people represented in this book who are no longer alive.

The interviews averaged about an hour, the shortest being about forty minutes and the longest almost two hours. Couples interviewed together took about ninety minutes.

Of the over three hundred people interviewed women were more willing and available so they make up sixty-four percent compared to thirty-six percent men. Their ethnic decent was almost entirely European with twenty-seven percent born outside of North America, mostly Europe.

In terms of education, thirteen percent had below grade nine, twenty-six percent had between grade nine and eleven, nineteen percent completed grade twelve, thirty-one percent went on from high school to get some university, military, technical or other training, and eleven percent had a university degree or higher.

LEVEL OF EDUCATION
▎ 13% - Below Grade Nine
▎ 26% - Between Grade 9 – 11

▌ 19% - Grade 12 (Completed High school)
▌ 31% - Some training beyond high school
▌ 11% - University degree or higher

It was much more difficult than one would think to arrange interviews because many people were disinterested, too guarded, or just annoyed that I was asking. I am very thankful for the referrals and to those who agreed to take the time to speak with me because I was turned down by many groups and individuals.

Approximately one third of the people approached for an interview declined for various reasons, so I thanked them and moved on. Another approximately one third were guarded and asked many questions of me before agreeing to be interviewed, (One lady interviewed me before she would let me interview her). They then shared experiences and gave insights but only to their level of comfort. After agreeing to be interviewed, one lady was so guarded that at first she was resistant to answer a basic demographic question on how many times she had been married insisting that it was her private business. But within a few minutes of warm conversation she shared her complete life story in detail. The final one third of the people readily agreed and was willing to share most anything with enthusiasm. One lady proclaimed at the outset "My life is an open book. I have nothing to hide."

"My life is an open book. I have nothing to hide."

To all those who agreed to be interviewed I promised strict confidentiality, and all responses are presented anonymously. Everyone who was interviewed signed a release saying they were interviewed of their own free will and that I am free to use their statements anonymously as part of a published work. In keeping with the promise made, I do not use anyone's name and have excluded lengthy or overly specific details that might reveal someone's identity.

My goal was to get an intimate look into their lives as deeply as they were willing to go and do my best in that time to get a sense of the world from their vantage point. I wasn't looking for deep dark secrets, even though I got some, but insights into their experiences, and more importantly their interpretation of those experiences. Through a series of pointed and revealing questions I exceeded my expectation.

As for the actual interviewing process, some were impressive people who addressed my questions directly and shared their experiences. There were a few, however, that controlled the interview almost completely and pursued their own agenda despite the questions I asked. During the initial demographic questions, for example, I asked one person where he was born then didn't say another word for over ten minutes as he gave a detail laden family history and foreshadowed issues he would "get into later." During an interview with one couple, the husband talked virtually the whole time only allowing his wife the occasional comment before he cut back in. I eventually got some of her thoughts but only by directing the focus (and my body) toward her several times. Some other people were either unwilling or incapable of answering a straight question with a straight answer.

One lady complained after the interview that I didn't ask enough questions about the stories and details of people's lives. I explained to her, and others, that while I did want to hear some stories I wasn't so much interested in the details of the stories but the way in which those stories have affected their understanding of the world and their place in it. For example, if a woman worked very hard on the farm I didn't want extensive details about the hard work. Rather, I wanted to know how it affected her outlook and changed her life experience. There were people who volunteered far too much detail and information that distracted from what I was actually looking for. On the other hand, some people were the perfect interview focusing on the questions and answering them directly with the right amount of detail. I really appreciated those people.

This is not written as a self help book, but it can be if you choose to use it for that purpose. But it is much more, a human interest story with something for everyone. For the younger person there is a wealth of knowledge and insight into life's trials and triumphs from those who have lived them. For the not so young there are familiar stories about some of the struggles and joys that many had in common.

Forgive me if the book reads like a crudely arranged string of quotes at times, sometimes switching tense and person to avoid changing the quote.

But I want the people interviewed to speak in their own words, and because they are anonymous there is no need to differentiate the speakers. Every set of quotation marks represents a different speaker but that doesn't really much matter because they are anonymous. So although it is somewhat unorthodox, it worked well for me to string small quotes together to make a coherent sentence. I ask your indulgence to read for content rather than form.

Their stories and insights will make you laugh, make you cry and touch your heart and mind in some way. There will most certainly be something that strikes you and makes you rethink your own life to some degree. Hopefully a particular regret or experience recounted here will spark a reassessment for you or help enhance your life experience in some way.

Overall, this experience was a riveting insight into the private lives and thoughts of those who have lived between sixty-five and one hundred years, endured hardships and tried to make sense of this crazy world. My life was enriched by speaking with so many wonderful people and my hope is that you have a similar experience from reading about it. Enjoy.

CHAPTER 2

THE WORKING YEARS

WE'VE ALL HEARD THE FAMILIAR LINE from Shakespeare's play *As You Like It*, "All the world's a stage, and all the men and women merely players." This passage refers to seven stages of life and the role we typically play during those stages. But the one that profoundly shapes our adult persona is the work stage, which for most people spans over forty years. We typically begin our work stage by imagining ourselves accepting and then fulfilling a certain role in order to make a living. And although our work might change throughout our lives every job begins with a willingness to adopt a particular persona for the role we accept.

Because we spend so much of our adult lives working there is little wonder that it has such a profound effect on shaping who we are. We grow into the role we assume which is reflected in the way we conduct ourselves, the confidence we develop from the skill and experience we achieve, our daily focus, and for some even our worldview. The knowledgeable teacher speaks carefully but with confidence, the policeman has an air of authority and responsibility, the nurse is a capable and willing caregiver, and the skilled carpenter has confidence doing tasks most would find difficult or impossible. The salesman speaks smoothly and becomes professionally sociable, the Pastor dresses modestly as he develops a kind and loving demeanor, and the mechanic on an oil rig becomes hard and tough with rough hands, a leathery face and a husky voice. And while there are exceptions and personality differences, we expect people of certain professions to act in predictable ways.

What someone does for a living is a primary identifier and often the first way we describe someone. In history we learn about the blacksmith, the soldier, the farmer, the newspaper editor and the judge. It provides us an instant frame of reference to know what someone did for a living, what role they assumed and what part they played in society. That's why it is one of the first questions asked about someone when we want to know more about them. And this is the primary reason why after some basic demographic questions I decided to start my research by asking about each person's work life. I was curious to know how people came to choose their work, how it shaped their lives and how they see it looking back.

I was fortunate to interview people who held a wide variety of jobs including trade and technical workers, homemakers, office workers, health care professionals, sales people, teachers, business owners, laborers, factory workers, managers, bankers, law enforcement and military people, farmers, and so on.

Some simply fell into a job and accepted the role they were given while others made a conscious choice to become what they wanted to be. Some people moved around often and switched jobs numerous times throughout their working years while others had the same profession or worked for the same company for their entire working life.

Because my primary focus was to gain insights in to what brings about a meaningful and fulfilling life I was most curious about whether or not people found their work life enjoyable and fulfilling. Some were even still working into their seventies and eighties which was impressive and inspirational.

There was one person, however, who had no comment on whether she enjoyed her work life. Imagine my surprise when I asked a lovely ninety-one year old lady what she did for work and she looked at me aghast (as though I had said the other four letter word) and said "Work? Heavens, I have never worked a day in my life. I was a totally spoiled kid that never wanted for anything. I had rich parents and maids. I hardly ever washed a dish and never washed a floor." She was prim and proper but not, as one might expect, overly haughty. She had accepted her role as a child of wealth and then a woman of privilege and seemed quite tolerable in it, even funny. I thoroughly enjoyed my interview with her.

"Work? Heavens, I have never worked a day in my life."

As I began to question people about their work and their likes and dislikes, I had no expectation. I assumed that some people wouldn't have liked their work but simply held their nose and went to work looking forward to the day they could retire. I assumed that others would be fifty-fifty on their job, didn't really like it but didn't really dislike it either. I further assumed that there would be people who enjoyed their work. What I didn't expect is that of the hundreds of people interviewed only three percent said they didn't like their job, eight percent said they were fifty-fifty, and eighty-nine percent said they enjoyed their work, and of those many said they loved it. The overwhelming majority said they got a great deal of meaning and fulfillment from their work.

I wondered out loud during some interviews if time had perhaps faded the memory of many of the difficulties and dislikes of work, but based on their responses I concluded that selective memory factored in very little. Those asked directly said it wasn't a factor and as I questioned deeper what they liked best and least about their work the likes far outweighed the dislikes in number and description. Thirty-two percent of those interviewed said there was nothing they really disliked about their work or had no response even after being asked a second time to think of something.

TOP TEN DISLIKES ABOUT WORK
▌ 1. Long hours, shifts
▌ 2. Bosses, management, union
▌ 3. Very hard work, pressure, responsibility
▌ 4. Some co-workers
▌ 5. Low pay
▌ 6. Some customers
▌ 7. Being away from home
▌ 8. Getting up early
▌ 9. Commuting
▌ 10. Feeling like a number

Of the three percent who said they didn't enjoy their work some people felt they were in a job that didn't suit them. One lady in sales said she did not enjoy dealing with the public and just wasn't a sales person. She lamented leaving a job she held earlier in life that suited her much better. Some small business owners also complained about dealing with a difficult public along with long hours, low wages, lack of benefits, pension or job security, and the constant pressure and struggle of being self employed. For some the burden of being married to a business undermined their job satisfaction and over-shadowed the reward.

Others who didn't enjoy their work talked of many and varied jobs that were boring, uninspiring or had low wages. One person complained of a strict and mean boss who robbed her of job satisfaction while another office worker simply said she hated typing and should never have been in that job. Another lady was a homebody and simply didn't like being away from her home for long hours.

Several homemakers complained of being tied down and unable to fulfill their own aspirations. One lady said she felt constantly controlled by others while another said she simply did not like domestic work. The most poignant example came from a lady who said she was completely unprepared to be a homemaker and mother. "I was a very poor child and starved, married at eighteen with no guidance or preparation and very little education." It's little wonder she disliked her working years as a homemaker.

"I was a very poor child and starved, married at eighteen with no guidance or preparation and very little education."

Twenty percent of the people interviewed were full time homemakers at one time and the majority of them were very satisfied with their role. But others complained of feeling alone at times, having no vehicle, being bored and feeling unappreciated. Farm wives were united in speaking of long hours, cold winters and a very hard life. One lady was married at seventeen and felt she lost her single life and the chance to learn about herself and her place in the world before being thrust into the role of looking after others.

Along with disliking the relentless nature of housework, numerous homemakers spoke of the difficulty of managing the chaos, disciplining children, paying bills, as well as keeping the family in food and clothing. Winters were long and housebound kids were also a problem for some. This was especially difficult for families with many children, some had as many as ten. One lady told of constant surprises and financial difficulties from her alcoholic husband who created many problems for a stay at home mom with five kids. Some families also had the added pressure of looking after cranky parents while raising children.

Some office workers complained of low pay and feeling they were being taken for granted. Others didn't enjoy typing or filing or just found office work boring. One person said that it was difficult managing an office with sixteen women and dealing with the issues related to each one's "time of the month." Another office worker complained of petty office gossip, racial differences and the resulting cliques that developed. Yet another complained that younger people didn't work as hard as the older workers.

Teachers had relatively high job satisfaction but were united in their dislikes regarding supervising (or babysitting) students, as well as coping with problem kids and kids on drugs. Some teachers of young children had difficultly at times managing the children and being consistent with discipline. Several teachers disliked grading papers and another spoke of the difficulties in dealing with some parents.

Nurses and health care professionals also had a high rate of job satisfaction and were hesitant to state any dislikes about their chosen vocation. But what was different with them is that unlike most dislikes, which had to do with the personal preferences, health-care-professionals spoke of the difficulties in seeing others suffer.

One lady said that as a young nurse in England at the end of WWII she was terribly affected by the condition of the young men returning from concentration camps, many of whom died upon their return as well as others who had lost limbs, were deathly skinny, seriously ill from malnutrition and disease, and missing teeth and fingernails. Another young nurse was terribly saddened by working with kids who were terminally ill, knowing there was no hope and they wouldn't recover. Yet another nurse had a difficult time working with young unwed mothers and watching them struggle as they gave up their babies for adoption, and a maternity nurse spoke of the pain of seeing parents lose a baby at birth.

Some nurses also complained of low pay, work stress from the pressure of being responsible for lives, long hours and shift work. Surprisingly there were also some complaints about rude and abusive patients. One would think that a nurse is like an angel to a sick person in the hospital, but apparently that is not always the case.

Some technical and trade workers spoke of the pressure to produce at a certain rate along with long hours, shift work, and cold winters. Many of them worked outside in extremely cold conditions on the Prairies. This was made even more difficult for some by being on call, solving tough problems and being away from home for extended periods in remote locations such as mines, pipelines or work camps.

Others complained of a time when there was an overall lack of safety precautions on job sites and they were forced to work in unsafe conditions. Potential workplace hazards were often coupled with breathing dust and chemicals. Physical problems were also exacerbated for many by constant hard labor that took its toll on their body and resulted in many long term health problems. It's not surprising that various physical ailments hampered some in their job, and more than one person complained that certain co-workers didn't work hard enough which was a serious issue on a physically demanding job.

Other dislikes worth mentioning had more to do with the person than the job. Many people lamented the difficulty of juggling work and life issues, making money, raising kids and trying to do well at both. Often one or both suffered as either work absorbed too much energy causing neglect of the family or family issues interfered with work responsibilities. On a related note one lady was discriminated against when in 1945 and again in 1954 was forced to leave her job because she was married and the company thought she would soon be having children and become a homemaker.

More than one person said they were unhappy with their level of success in their occupation and felt they should have done better. Another person wished he had been more sociable at work rather than being gruff and keeping to himself so much, and another admitted that his poor attitude hampered him in his job. Several people also felt that because work required so much time and energy they were not able to pursue other interests or do the things they might have preferred.

For all the dislikes that people voiced there were some who were indifferent to work but just accepted their lot. It was unfulfilling but paid the bills so for them dispassion bred acceptance as they fulfilled their role with indifference until retirement. But the overwhelming majority of people said they enjoyed their work and were more than happy to talk about it.

Some people had a good idea of what they wanted to be and pursued a specific profession choosing to be a pilot, nurse, tradesman, etc. Others just fell into a job by accident or happenstance. But whether someone chose a specific job or simply fell into a vocation seemed to make little difference in overall job satisfaction. This may be due, at least in part, to the fact that the top ten reasons people gave for high job satisfaction could apply to virtually any vocation.

TOP TEN LIKES ABOUT WORK

1. Enjoy People, customers, coworkers, etc.
2. Helping others
3. Challenging, hard work
4. Making money and paying bills
5. Interesting
6. Freedom, no desk, own boss
7. Variety
8. Sense of accomplishment
9. Had a natural ability for it
10. Learning things

The number one answer when asked what people liked most about their job was "the people," coworkers, customers, and associates. This is very telling because it indicates that in many ways the people meant more than the job. For some there was a "family atmosphere, good treatment, and good working conditions." Others spoke fondly about "the gang of people I worked with," and "all the girls; we had fun." Many people developed a respect for those they met at work that provided a great deal of satisfaction and in some cases formed lifelong friendships.

Helping others was the next most popular response and gave many people a great deal of satisfaction in their work. For some it was "looking after elderly people," while for others it was "meeting people, and being involved in the community." An optometrist was proud to say "I knew what I was doing helped people to see better," and a person in search and rescue said "I helped lots of people and made a big difference."

"I helped lots of people and made a big difference."

Many people were happy that their work was challenging and spoke of a certain invigoration and satisfaction that comes with doing a job that involves some challenge and struggle. For some it was "hard work, crews," "working with my hands," and "the challenge of making the equipment work." For a medical lab technician it was "the challenge of finding out what made people ill," and for a manager it was "being responsible for all the grain cars" at two international ports.

What some people liked most about their job was simply making money and paying bills. For them it was as simple as being able to generate money to sustain their family, "providing for everyone," or "just surviving."

Having a job that was interesting and allowed creativity was important to many people while for others it was a sense of freedom that made their job enjoyable. Several people were happy not to be "tied to a desk," and a truck driver described his job as flexible as he enjoyed the "freedom of the road," saying "I could get away." Many people also agreed with one man who said "I was my own boss."

Routine is comfortable for some and torturous for others, so for many people freedom in their job involved "scope, variety, no limit," "adventure," and "something different all the time." One engineer loved that he "travelled on an expense account," along with all the variety involved as every situation was different. Another person only stayed at jobs until he tired and said "I changed jobs when I needed a change."

A sense of accomplishment was key for many people such as those who built things, carried out important tasks, lived up to responsibilities and just generally did a good job at whatever their vocation. Several homemakers talked about "being needed," and a farm wife looked at survival and raising a family as a significant accomplishment.

Many people felt fortunate to be in a job for which they had a natural ability and affinity. One person said of his job "I had a natural bent for it," and another said "I have a knack for machine work." A bookkeeper said "I was excellent at math so it was a natural job for me," and a farmer said "I like to be around cows."

Several sales people felt a natural connection in their job saying things like "I loved selling, loved people and studying human nature," "I'm a people person, I like people," and "it was an outlet for my creativity." An entertainer said "I had natural talent and enjoyed lots of good experiences, travelling, meeting people," and a sailor said "I loved the sea and big waves, bigger the better, and never got sea sick."

Another popular response to the most liked aspects of work was "learning something new all the time." As one person put it "I could always learn so was never in a dead end." One person who changed jobs several times through his life liked the fact that he "learned something new at every job." For another person it was just as important "learning about what not to do too," and another added "my job enabled me to understand human nature."

"I could always learn so was never in a dead end."

Some people offered more insights about particular jobs including homemakers who were very forthright in saying what they liked about their job, giving birth to their children then watching them grow. They were rewarded by being able to give the children a good start, teach them life principles, be there for them after school and keep them safe. One lady said "I was just happy being where my kids were." When asked if they felt like they missed out on anything, most of them said no. One mom said she always felt like she was doing the right thing and wouldn't have traded it for anything. Farm wives talked of the added hardships of farm life but added that there was a great satisfaction in working together to survive. Some also spoke fondly of the animals and fresh air.

"I was just happy being where my kids were."

Office workers who enjoyed their work spoke of the comfortable office environment, a warm and dry place where everything was organized. One lady said she just loved numbers and keeping everything in order. Another said she felt like she was part of something important while another said she was very happy in a support role and didn't need the spot light.

The opposite sentiment was expressed by an executive who enjoyed the profile and said that much of his job satisfaction came from his influence. He reveled in the fact that he could "do a lot for a lot of people." Another said that he really enjoyed the authority he had over his area of the company.

One salesperson saw herself as a people person who really enjoyed helping people make purchases, and another said he looked at his sales job like helping people solve problems. People would come to him looking for something they needed, and he would guide them to the best product for the best price. Others spoke of a certain thrill in making the sale while at the same time making people happy.

Teachers consistently had high job satisfaction as most said they loved teaching the children and helping them in times of need. One teacher said "I was proud of my job" while another said "I was the boss of the classroom." This echoes another teacher who said he "felt alive in front of the class." It was his stage where he could make a big difference in his students' lives. The summer vacations were also mentioned as a perk of the job by more than one teacher.

Like teachers, health care professionals also expressed a high level of job satisfaction through helping people and making a significant difference in their lives. They all spoke of feeling like they were doing something important. A maternity nurse brimmed as she spoke about sharing the joy with families as they brought new life into the world, and another lady was quite frank in saying that she always felt there was a romantic notion to being a nurse.

This was similar to those in the military, police force and search and rescue who felt a certain prestige to their vocation and were all proud to play a vital role in society. One said "I felt like I was doing my part and loved the responsibility." This was reiterated by another who spoke of his high level of satisfaction by receiving significant military postings while having the opportunity to visit more than eighty countries and make a significant dif-ference in the lives of many people around the world.

Trade and technical people had many and varied experiences but all had satisfaction in some way working with their hands and producing things. One contractor spoke of the exhilaration of seeing a picture of something then making it appear in front of them as they built it. Many tradesman and technical workers also enjoyed moving around to different locations to work and some expressed how much they enjoyed working outdoors.

Several tradesmen expressed tremendous personal satisfaction at hav-ing a natural ability as well as the training to do something better than most other people. One person enjoyed the challenge and success of being competent at many trades saying that he was just trying to show people he wasn't stupid even though he had very little formal education. Another enjoyed the challenge of making equipment work saying "I had a knack for machine work, was good at it and fast." This was a common feeling as many trade and technical workers spoke of the satisfaction they got from building things and solving tough problems for people.

Overall I was very impressed with the work ethic of the people inter-viewed and many spoke of the satisfaction they got from any kind of work. One impressive man simply said "I just loved working hard" and found it invigorating to work on a fishing boat, build things, or chop wood. Others said work made them feel utilized and engaged giving them a sense of pur-pose. Work keeps the mind busy and gives us something to do, something we all need.

"I just loved working hard."

As I processed all the things people told me about work an irony emerged. Some of the same responses were given as both likes and dislikes. Some people thought it was a perk to travel for their work while others disliked too much travel. Some really liked being outside and others didn't. Some people enjoyed pressure and responsibility while others avoided it. One person said his greatest like was being his own boss yet his greatest dislike was also being his own boss. Some housewives said they felt tied down being at home all the time while others said how free they felt to be home with the kids and also have time to pursue their own interests. Some housewives said they disliked the chaos of constant surprises while others found it exhilarating. There were office workers who enjoyed their environment as safe and comfortable while others found it boring and constricting. The indication is that it is one's view and preference that largely determines the level of work satisfaction and enjoyment.

Based on the top ten reasons people found fulfillment in their work, below is the list of questions anyone could ask to achieve a higher level of job satisfaction. If you can answer yes to most of these questions you should be able to achieve the kind of job satisfaction that almost ninety percent of the people interviewed expressed.

TOP TEN QUESTIONS TO ASK FOR JOB SATISFACTION.

1. Do you enjoy people, coworkers, bosses, customers, associates?
2. Do you have a sense that you're helping others in your work?
3. Do you find your work challenging in some way?
4. Do you feel satisfaction that you're making money and paying bills?
5. Do you find your work interesting in some way?
6. Do you have a sense of freedom in your job, physical, mental or creative?
7. Is there some variety to your work?
8. Do you feel a sense of accomplishment in your work?
9. Do you have a natural ability for what you're doing?
10. Are you learning things at your work?

For virtually everyone work is an integral part of the human experience, and far from being a burden most people interviewed genuinely enjoyed it. Regardless of the type of work or particular vocation, most people learned to enjoy it and work hard at it. One person even said he never had a job he didn't like. Perhaps this is because work brings challenge and accomplishment together in a way that builds character and confidence that we can't get anywhere else. And because it is such a large part of life and necessary to sustain ourselves it provides a great deal of life's meaning.

It's inspirational to know that looking back on their work lives the over-whelming majority of people over the age of sixty-five remember it fondly. This means that young people can look forward to a great deal of fulfillment in their work not to mention years of good experiences and meaningful interaction with others.

CHAPTER 3

LIFESTYLES

TO GET A BETTER SENSE of the people interviewed and gain more in-sights into their various lifestyles during their early and working years, I asked a series of questions including whether they moved a lot, owned a home, how much they travelled, whether they were involved in any clubs or organizations, and whether they practiced a religion.

I was curious how often people moved and how it affected their lives so I asked simply whether they moved a lot (meaning frequently or every few years during their working years) or whether they stayed mostly in one place (meaning ten or more years in the same house during that time). Sixty-two percent said they lived mostly in one place while working and raising a family, and many spoke fondly of having a home base. One lady who is now well in to her eighties still lives in the same house by herself. Most others now live in townhomes, apartments or care homes but were happy to speak of their long term family home. Some wished out loud that they were still there.

Thirty-two percent of respondents said they moved a lot. For some peo-ple jobs, homes, and even cities, changed frequently. This was especially true of those in the military, police force, banks, trades or any vocation where changing location was an integral part of the job. Others seemed to be habitual movers and one lady reluctantly admitted she couldn't count how many times they moved and that they lived "all over the place."

But whether a family moved frequently or not had little bearing on home ownership because for most people houses were bought and sold as part of the moving process. Ninety-four percent said they were able to own a home during their working years and beyond. Generally those who stayed mostly in one place in a home that they owned felt they had a more secure and stable environment for their growing family. They expressed more of a sense of roots. However, this should not disparage those who provided well for their families but were forced to move frequently by the circumstances of work and life.

I asked people if they took a lot of holidays or travelled much and the answers were varied and sometimes surprising. There were three categories beginning with those who travelled very little and took virtually no holidays. The second group includes those who had a holiday each year and travelled somewhat but not extensively, and the final group includes those who travelled extensively to many places around the globe.

To my surprise a full twenty-seven percent, over one in four people interviewed, said that for most of their lives and through the years of working and raising a family they had virtually no time or money for leisure travel or holidays. The reasons were many and varied including one person who said he has never been overseas and travelled all over North America but only through his work as a bus driver. He travelled extensively but took almost no holidays and did very little sightseeing as he was busy driving. This was echoed by several other people who said they travelled quite a bit for work but didn't take holidays because money and time were always tight.

More than a few people had little interest in holidays. One lady said with resignation that her husband wasn't interested in holidays so they hardly went anywhere. On a more negative note, another lady facetiously said her master, meaning her very controlling husband, wouldn't take her anywhere. Yet there were some who simply said they loved being at home anyway and didn't really care to go anywhere else.

For some it was a matter of being frugal and avoiding debt. They might have liked to travel more but didn't want to spend the money. Another lady said that her family had no time or money for holidays but that they lived by a nice lake and had a boat so their home was their holiday and she never felt like she missed out.

Some people didn't travel much because of responsibilities. Many who owned a small business and worked over sixty hours per week throughout the entire year felt they couldn't leave for any substantial holidays. This was also true for many farmers who said that they not only didn't have the money but couldn't leave their responsibilities. One farmer just said with acceptance "we worked on the farm, always."

"We worked on the farm, always."

Along with finding the time and money, large families had logistical problems that severely hindered them from taking significant holidays. Two people interviewed had ten kids which would have required a bus just to transport the family. It's almost unimaginable for most people to have that size of a family and yet more than fifty percent of those interviewed had three or more children, and many of those families had stay at home moms and lived on one income. So it's easy to see that travel or holidays would be difficult.

Other reasons for lack of holidays include insufficient time off work. One man reminded me that many years ago not everyone had enough time off work to take much of a holiday and that for many years he was only given one week per year from his job. Coupled with a modest salary and big family, holidays were not a viable option for many people. One lady added that she was from a very large family and grew up in boarding schools so almost never took family holidays.

Several people said that family illness prevented holidays. One lady said her mom was sick virtually the whole time she was growing up so the family had no opportunity to take holidays or travel. Another lady said her husband was sick for many years so she was forced to support him and their four children, and another person said she was too sick over an extended period with heart defects and surgeries to take any holidays. Overall it was very sobering to think that so many people's life circumstance didn't allow the opportunity to take at least modest holidays or travel.

Thirty-three percent of respondents said they took modest holidays, maybe one per year. As expected the most common response was taking camping trips, which were a relatively inexpensive getaway for families with lots of kids and lack of money. Many people smiled as they spoke fondly about family camping trips, and some were fortunate enough to have a boat or motorhome. Others spoke of visiting relatives so that they had a place to stay, and more than one person said they would visit relatives back on the farm for a few weeks each summer. And although it was a nice getaway back to nature and animals, that holiday invariably involved some work. Driving trips and sightseeing day trips were also a popular choice for many who were on a budget and needed to stay close to home.

Some families were able to use sports to travel on a budget with at least some family members. Many spoke of scout trips, sports trips or other club trips that were sponsored by an organization.

Given that twenty-seven percent took virtually no holidays and thirty-three percent took modest holidays, only forty percent of those who responded took numerous holidays and travelled extensively, but it should be noted that some of these were after the family had grown and time and resources were more available. Those who were able to travel during their working years usually had some provision that made it possible. If both partners worked the family often had specified holidays from work and made enough money to afford it so significant holidays were possible.

One person said her dad was a ship captain so she travelled extensively with him at times, and another lady's husband was also a ship captain so she saw much of the world. Others spoke of being able to take advantage of travel opportunities by having a close relative who was an airline pilot, worked for the airlines, or worked for the railroad.

A number of people travelled on expense accounts. One lady was thrilled that her husband travelled extensively for work and she had the opportunity to go with him and sightsee while he was busy at his job. For her it was a chance to see the world for free. Others were also able to mix work and holidays in a way that satisfied both. When asked about travelling and holidays one lady simply said "my whole life was a holiday. I've travelled everywhere." In fact several people said they have "been everywhere," some of whom were in the navy or other armed forces stationed around the globe and who took extensive holidays as well. There were also those who were born in Europe and took regular trips back to see family, sometimes for extended periods.

"My whole life was a holiday. I've travelled everywhere."

For some people travel was a passion and one lady laughingly said "wanderlust is a family trait." One person who has enjoyed over twenty cruises after her children were grown said that if she had her way she would live on a cruise ship year round. A widow said that she and her husband had been to Hawaii thirty-two times over the years and loved it there, while another couple boasted they had visited over one hundred countries. Overall, those who travelled extensively made it a priority and simply found the resources to do it. For some that meant extensive trips in their motorhome or extended periods at a cottage, and for others it meant finding the ways and means to visit many overseas destinations.

Another aspect of people's lifestyles that I was curious about was what type of clubs, organizations or charity work they were involved in. I was casual in the way I asked and didn't press for an extensive list from anyone and therefore it is somewhat incomplete. But my goal was to get an impression of how people viewed being involved in groups and organizations and in that respect I succeeded. I broke it down to three general categories, 1) those who were not involved in any organizations; 2) those that joined one or two; and 3) those that joined three or more.

One third of those interviewed said they didn't join clubs. The reasons were quite simple as some didn't have the time or money, some just preferred keep to themselves, and many others simply said "I'm not a joiner." Not surprisingly many people said they were too busy with work and family to join any outside groups. One lady said that with so many children and being so short of time and money there was no time to join anything. Another lady said that her husband was too sick and she was too isolated to have the opportunity to join any groups. On a more comical note one man listed off four clubs he belonged to over the years then followed up by saying "I wasn't a joiner." I didn't query him further. When I asked an Irish truck driver if he was involved in any clubs, organizations or charity work he laughingly answered "yes, gangs and jail. I was a wild kid."

Forty percent of those interviewed were involved in one or two clubs or organizations and twenty-seven percent said they were involved in a number of clubs, three or more. It is encouraging to think that over seventy percent of the people interviewed belonged to some kind of organization at some point in their lives, many of which had a positive social value. The types of organizations people were involved is quite broad but I attempt to group them into discernable categories.

Topping the list were those involved in some type of community based organization which might include a social help group, hospice, as well as other groups such as a community choirs or local theatre. Many people found such organizations attractive because they were not only inexpensive and accessible but also had a tangible social value.

The next most popular response came from those involved in some kind of sports organization. This might include playing sports as a child or playing, coaching or volunteering for a sports group as an adult. A surprising number of seniors were still very much involved in many age-appropriate sports clubs such as golf, tennis, lawn bowling, and so on. It was inspiring that most people were still involved in sports related social activities as much as they were able. A very inspiring and spry one hundred year old man said he coached boxing well in to his eighties.

Third in most popular responses were those who were members of lodges, fraternities or sororities, and many people were proud to have been involved in a club or lodge such as Kinsmen, Rotary, Beta Sigma Phi, Lions, Masons, Job's Daughters, and many more.

A close fourth were those involved in the Scouts and Guides, 4H and YMCA groups. Many people had fond memories of such groups from their youth, and many adults also became involved as leaders or parent volunteers.

Next in popular responses were work related groups such as unions, professional clubs or other organizations that grew out of a work place. This was followed closely by those involved in school organizations such as the Parent Teachers Association (P.T.A), parent volunteers, and other groups related to schooling children.

Not surprisingly there were people who were members of Sunday school groups and church boards, political and social activist organizations, Legions and veterans groups, as well as Cadets or the Army Reserves. More than a few people were members of Toast Masters and other self improvement groups as well as AA and Al Anon. Most spoke of the positive impact it had on their lives.

I interviewed some Red Hat Ladies who were particularly willing to laugh at themselves and seem to have a pact to be cheerful. Others were enthused to be part of music groups such as the barber shop quartets and the operatic society. Music also provided some people a means to put on events, and one person glowingly spoke of the opportunity he had to entertain the troops during WWII.

There were also those in the horticultural society, bird watching clubs, book clubs, genealogy clubs and even quilting clubs, something that would seem so outdated to young people now. Some were members of clubs rarely heard of such as heraldry (the study of coats of arms and history of old families), vexillology (the study of flags), and the Pot and Kettle Club for those in the hardware business. There were also a few who boasted of being part of exclusive clubs for the wealthy, country clubs, yacht clubs and other such elite organizations. Quite a few people were also involved in singles clubs including Parents Without Partners, Singles Over Sixty, and Flying Solo.

The most comical group described was the Cheerful Chubbies weight loss club. A group of robust ladies who were ostensibly trying to lose weight would meet periodically and place a big pig in the middle of the table. Those who had gained weight or were the same since their previous meeting would have to put ten cents into the pig. When it was full they would buy Chinese food for everyone. It sounded more like a fun social group than a serious weight loss club, hence the name 'Cheerful Chubbies.'

Some people supported one or maybe two organizations while others listed as many as five or more, but overall most people spoke fondly of their associations with such groups and the fulfillment they got from being a member of something they felt was worthy of their time and resources. Most of these groups added something to the community and enhanced the lives of others in some way. One lady simply said "I always volunteered for things."

"I always volunteered for things."

In exploring people's lifestyles I was also curious how many people practiced a religion and to what extent. Given the older generation I assumed the positive responses would be quite high, especially for Sunday school. But I made no value judgment and asked for no explanation, even though some people felt the need to explain why they fell away from church after their childhood. There were essentially three groups, 1) those who did not practice a religion at all; 2) those that had an affiliation at one time and retained some form of belief but attended less than twice per year; and 3) those that practiced a religion and attended with some regularity, more than twice per year.

Twenty-four percent of the people interviewed said they did not practice a religion at all. Many did not even go to Sunday school, which is somewhat surprising given its prevalence during the earlier part of the twentieth century. One lady boldly proclaimed "I'm a heathen." Others stated that they were against any kind of organized religion, and another said he "tried a bunch of religious views and practices but didn't like any of them."

"I'm a heathen."

More than one person said they did not practice any religion but were adamant that they believe in God. A few people said they have a personal faith between them and their maker but don't practice any public faith and don't talk about it. Along the same line of reasoning, another person said that he's tried everything and decided that "nature is God's church." Others were indifferent about religion and one person simply said he wasn't for it or against it.

Twelve percent of respondents said they practiced a religion somewhat. They may have been raised in a particular church and still feel some connection but haven't practiced it since childhood, or they may attend periodically for a specific occasion. Such people may go to church on some special occasions such as Christmas, or Easter, and they willingly participate in weddings and funerals as carried out by a religious group. But more than a few people said they were forced to participate in their parents' religion and as a result had "too much religion" when they were younger. One person complained that when he was younger his whole family revolved around the church. As a result, many people said they practiced a religion when younger but not later. Conversely, some others said they practiced religion when younger by force and later by choice.

Sixty-four percent of those interviewed practiced a religion and attended some form of services more than twice per year. Contrary to those who went to Sunday school and didn't practice any religion after, many people came back to religious belief and practice later in life. Still others who had not been raised in the church discovered a religious faith later in life.

For those who regularly practiced a faith, some were on and off all of their lives but never lost a connection with their church while others were raised in a particular denomination and consistently treated it as part of their life. This may be due to the fact that many children were socialized in a particular church and felt a strong connection and sense of belonging. One lady was adamant in saying she was "a Lutheran by birth," and many people spoke of the Church of England with a certain pride and ownership. When I asked some Brits who said they practiced a faith what denomination they were affiliated with, most answered with an odd look as if to say "the Church of England, of course." Certain denominations seem adept at breeding an affinity in their parishioners that lasts virtually unquestioned for life. The Catholic Church and Orthodox Churches also seem to have faithful and lifelong parishioners.

There were also many Protestants who were consistent in practicing their faith throughout their lives. Some were socialized in a particular denomination and had parents or relatives who were deeply involved in church as lay leaders, evangelists, lay pastors or gospel singers. Along with the community of church goers to which they belonged, this created a lifelong bond for many, even though many Protestants seemed much more flexible with denominations and some casually listed several churches they attended. Some, but not many, even switched from Roman Catholic to Protestant and vice versa.

Unlike those who sincerely practiced a spiritual religious faith, there were those who focused more on the social aspect of church as a place for nice people and friends to be together and either minimized or avoided the spiritual aspect. One lady said she practiced a religion and named a church affiliation but also described herself as a liberal and said she didn't like the

sermons much. For her, and some others, religious affiliation doesn't necessarily mean an inner religious experience or even belief in the divine for
that matter.

Others grew tired of church dogma and expanded their view beyond
the exclusiveness of Christianity to include a variety of beliefs. Some told
of their journey from the dogmatic beliefs of traditional religion to a more
inclusive "spiritual" approach to the divine. A leader in one particular denomination said they have done away with the idea of God as Santa Claus
and adjusted their beliefs to eliminate dogma, rules and ritual. For them this
created a church full of nice, spiritual people who are very inclusive and
open in what they believe.

Several others spoke of their journey through several Protestant denominations to a Buddhist faith or past lives and regression. Several people had
done regression work and one person went into detail about the various
people she used to be in previous lives. Another person shared her beliefs
then offered me tarot and palm readings as well as a numerology chart after
the interview.

Combining those who were marginal followers with those who were
more involved in a religion, seventy-six percent of the people interviewed
acknowledged some religious affiliation. The overwhelming majority was
Protestant but there were also many Catholics, two Jehovah's Witnesses, two
Mormons, two Buddhists, one Greek Orthodox, one non-religious Jew, and
six people who just described themselves as spiritual.

CHAPTER 4

THE HARDEST THING YOU'VE EVER DEALT WITH

WE ALWAYS LIKE to hear warm and fuzzy stories about how great life is, and during the course of my interviews I heard some. But for most people that is not the full story. Seeking life lessons from people who had worked through hardships, I was anxious to ask about the most difficult events or times of their lives. Answers ranged from one person who simply said he thrived under pressure yet gave no examples of difficulties to a lady who willingly elaborated on events that made her whole life very difficult. Some offered only one answer while others listed as many as five, but the vast majority experienced some very tragic and difficult circumstances at times in life. For a few people their life was one long series of tragedy and difficulty from the beginning.

TOP TEN HARDEST THINGS
YOU'VE EVER HAD TO DEAL WITH?

1. Death of a spouse, child, family, friends
2. Seeing loved ones sick or injured
3. Loss of health, cancer, disease, debilitation
4. Financial loss of job or investment
5. Divorce
6. Raising kids, supporting family
7. Family drug and alcohol problems
8. WWII, war
9. Childhood trauma, Family breakup
10. Farm work, hard work / The Great Depression

In many ways this was the most difficult chapter to write because of all the heartache it contains. The common theme was loss of some kind. Almost fifty percent of those interviewed had suffered the loss of a spouse, a shocking eleven percent had lost a child, and everyone had lost significant loved ones. There were stories of childhood trauma, disease, and family breakup from separation and divorce. People spoke of the difficulties of sustaining a large family, the pain of watching loved ones sick and suffering, many forms of abuse, mental illness, and drug and alcohol problems. Still others spoke of job loss, personal and family displacement, backbreaking work in order to survive, moving to a new country, and being away from home for extended periods. This was compounded for many by the Great Depression, World War II and other war related hardships.

This all sounds quite unsettling but keep in mind that I asked people about the most difficult events and circumstances in their lives and recount many of them here. While it was clear to me that some were still reliving them, most had dealt with them emotionally. Considering the revelations in the following pages, it is inspiring to think that most people were able to come to terms with the hardships they suffered.

Almost fifty percent of those interviewed had lost their life partner, which is perhaps not surprising given their advanced age. But this was their longest and most intimate relationship and for almost everyone their most devastating loss. Most people just responded without hesitation that it was the hardest thing they ever had to deal with and left it at that. Some offered insights on the shock of losing a spouse prematurely, but for most their focus was the emptiness and resulting loneliness they felt.

One lady recounted how her husband was killed at work in an industrial accident leaving her to care for three teenage boys, while another spoke of the loneliness she felt when her husband died unexpectedly while she was recovering from a serious car accident in which she had broken her back. Another widower recounted how with three young kids to look after his wife was injured and remained in a coma for sixteen years before she died.

For most people it was the pain of losing a spouse later in life that was their most difficult time. One lady said she has had tremendous difficulty coping on her own since her husband died and another said it has been a few years since her husband died and she's "still not over it."

One widower said that when his wife died he moved out of the apartment they had lived in and left it untouched for six years just paying the rent and visiting it periodically. Another said he simply lost interest in everything and just kept to himself for many years and has only recently begun to engage the world again.

Other tragic stories include the man whose elderly wife fell down the stairs of their family home, broke her neck and died shortly after. A particularly touching story came from a man who was devastated at the death of his second wife who he described as the true love of his life. He scattered her ashes on a local mountain and waves to her with love every time he drives by.

For one widow the tragedy of losing her husband was compounded by losing a child at the same time. Her husband and son had built an airplane which crashed and killed both of them. Another lady whose twenty year old son drowned and husband died shortly after said with resignation "everyone has died on me."

"Everyone has died on me."

For most people the thought of losing a child is devastating, not only because there is an expectation that the parent will die first but parents feel a tremendous responsibility for the lives of their children. Eleven percent of those interviewed had lost a child, a number that far exceeded my expectation and seems exorbitantly high. I suppose I just thought it doesn't happen very often and was perhaps naïve about how many people live with such pain. Having interviewed over three hundred people it stung every time I asked someone about their greatest hardship and they said they had lost a child. I could sense their pain, like a dagger in the heart that can never be pulled out and remains a dull ache, whether they lost a child at birth, in their formative years or as adults.

One lady described her most difficult time as having a 'blue baby' who lived a short time after birth then died. The most tragic time for one man was watching his five year old daughter die of a disease and then dealing with the helplessness he felt at not being able to save her. Another couple suffered the tragedy of losing their ten year old son in an accident at school, and one lady shared the pain of helping her fourteen year old son cope with cancer, spending the last ten days of his life with him then watching him die. Another lady experienced a compound tragedy when after losing her eighteen year old son in an accident said the toughest part was keeping her husband from going down the drain from depression and alcohol.

One couple had to endure the pain of losing a nineteen year old son who was injured in a car accident and remained in a coma for twelve years before he died. They both expressed how difficult it was trying to maintain hope all those years while coping with the pain and grief experienced by his two brothers. Another man, well into his eighties, recounted the pain of losing his son at age twenty who died in a fishing accident when his hip waders filled up with water. He said he could never understand why God would take their only child when he and his wife had centered their whole life on him. His wife was devastated, somehow thinking it was her fault, and has since passed on as well. He lives the rest of his days in lament.

Others shared tragic details of the death of a child like one lady who said she was suicidal after her son was killed by a drunk driver at age twenty-eight. Another relived the pain as she told of a son who was mildly handi-capped at birth, a problem child in every respect, manic depressive, continu-ously unemployed, had no money and committed suicide at age thirty-four. She admitted his death was tragic but also a relief because his life was so painful and he was so unhappy. A similar circumstance occurred for a lady whose son was involved in drugs and crime from his teen years well into his adult years, disappeared for seven years then committed suicide at age thirty-nine.

One dad shared the pain he still feels when his son, who he described as his best friend, died of a brain tumor at age thirty-four. Another lady had resigned herself to the loss of two adult daughters from disease, one in her late thirties and the other in her early forties.

Two stories that were especially moving include one lady who described how her step daughter was murdered by her ex-husband. The fear and help-lessness the family felt as their daughter was stalked and then murdered by her maniacal ex-husband added to the tragedy of losing her. And the most graphic and moving story came from a lady who said as her twenty-six year old son returned home from a hunting trip his gun accidentally went off as he exited his truck and he was killed. She was called to attend and when she arrived her son's body was under a tarp in his driveway. His blood flowed out from under the tarp as she spoke to authorities, numbed and overwhelmed by the situation.

To say that death is an inevitable part of life is small comfort for those who have lost loved ones, often under tragic circumstances. Many people listed the death of family members amongst the hardest circumstances they had to deal with, particularly parents and siblings. There were various reasons for this but some expressed a sense of security from their parents that died with them and others reflected on the warmth and friendship they had with their parents and siblings that they missed. A few people spoke fondly of the respect they had for how hard their parents struggled to raise the family and reflected on them with sadness after they were gone.

One lady said that the hardest thing she has had to deal with is missing all her family and friends that have died. There were numerous stories of compound tragedy including one lady who said she lost her husband and eleven family members in eighteen months. Another man told how he lost his wife, two sons and his parents, while another lost four siblings in two years. Surprisingly though, there wasn't a lot of complaining about the unfairness of it all, even from the two people whose sibling was murdered.

For many people the circumstances surrounding the unexpected death of loved ones added to the tragedy. One lady told how her dad was very sick in the hospital and as her mother drove home from visiting him was killed in a car accident. Then her dad died shortly after. Another man recounted how his betrothed and her dad were killed in a car accident the day before the formal marriage proposal. Tragedy continued for a lady who lost two brothers in their thirties by accidents and then her dad died on the operating table while getting his teeth removed. Holiday time was forever changed for another lady who lost two brothers right before Christmas. There were more such examples as death visited so many so often in cruel and unexpected ways.

For some the difficulty of dealing with death extended to animals as those who love them are often passionate and share a deep love of all living things. Many horse and dog lovers were very attached to their pets and expressed great difficulty at losing them. One lady said that having her cat put to sleep was the most difficult and traumatic event of her life.

Beyond the death of loved ones the most difficult time of life for many people was watching others suffer. Many people were forced to cope with a parent or spouse suffering with dementia and Alzheimer's. I interviewed one man while he held the hand of his wife of over fifty years as she stared straight ahead not knowing who he was. Many adult children experienced the same hardship with a once engaging parent whose mind and personality were lost.

Given that almost fifty percent of those interviewed were widowed many had cared for a spouse through illness to death. Some were in that position at the time of the interview. One man's ill wife was upstairs and too sick to join us for the interview. For others it was a long and arduous process as one lady said her husband was sick for forty years with heart attacks, cancer and a myriad of other problems. He couldn't work and the family thought he would die many times. Another woman spoke of the difficulties in caring for her "sick and incapacitated husband." One lady said with sadness that she was always looking after sick people.

For many people watching a child suffer was particularly devastating as one lady shared that seeing sick children suffer and die during her nurse's training was a life changing trauma. Many of them were terminally ill so there was nothing hopeful that could be thought or said to the family. For others it was watching their own children struggle with afflictions such as polio, cancer, heart problems, hearing problems, schizophrenia, and a myriad of other health problems. One lady said that the most difficult time in her life was when she had to put her eight year old epileptic son into an institution.

For others the pain of watching a loved one suffer came in various forms like the man who watched his daughter go through a painful divorce, or the heartache for one lady who helped her daughter through the trauma of losing a child at birth. One man's son was injured in a fight which he said required a long recovery and changed his personality.

Another woman whose daughter was raped related the pain of helping in her recovery then going through the difficult court process and putting her attacker in jail.

Health issues were named by many people as the most difficult issue of their lives. Loss of health had a profound effect on many, even changing their personality and undermining self confidence. One man was devastated when told that for health reasons he couldn't work in his trade anymore. That was all he knew, it gave him confidence, a means of support, a sense that he was contributing to society, and a professional camaraderie that was irreplaceable.

Many people battled with lifelong illness like one lady who shared that she has always been sickly from five years old and another who said she had suffered from constant illness all her life. Illness had a negative effect on many people's lives, but especially on their dreams, hopes and aspirations.

Others named serious injuries as their most difficult times such as a broken back, a broken hip, and a stroke. One lady suffered from polio earlier in life, had a serious car accident when she was seven months pregnant, and then lost her house from the resulting financial breakdown. Another lady suffered a broken back and many years of recovery when her chair lift at a ski hill detached and fell to the ground. The lady beside her died from the fall.

Not surprisingly many people suffered from cancer, and most were very candid about it. Some had beaten it, others were fighting it and one lady simply looked at me and said "I'm dying of terminal pancreatic cancer."

"I'm dying of terminal pancreatic cancer."

Breathing problems were also a major health issue and a number of people were permanently hooked up to oxygen. Heavy smoking was a primary contributor but also those who had worked in mines, factories and around asbestos without proper safety apparatus. One frail man in his eighties said he worked all his life but now is tied to his oxygen in a small room in his care home just "waiting to die."

Financial hardship was mentioned by many people as one of the most difficult issues in their lives. Many had lost sizeable amounts of money in investments which severely affected the financial security they had worked for. Personal bankruptcy was most difficult for one man while another lost most of his investments in 1982 when the interest rates soared into double digits. One business woman suffered hardship and a long recovery when an accountant embezzled a great deal of money from her company.

Far from losing investments, many people simply said that they were just always short of money. With large families and limited cash flow many people adopted a lifestyle of living with little or no money. This was especially accentuated by the Great Depression as I heard many stories of the tough times during the 1930s. Some were the age that they saw their parents struggle with no job, no money and few prospects, while others were old enough to be the parents who struggled. And although almost no one that I asked ever went to bed hungry, it was a time of tremendous struggle and uncertainty. A one hundred year old ex-pro boxer described how he jumped freight trains during the Depression and went to Prairie towns to put on boxing matches to make money. He summed it up by saying "it was a very tough life."

"It was a very tough life."

In many ways divorce is like a death, the death of a relationship and a family. Such loss was recounted by many people as one of the most difficult times of their lives, a time when their whole world was turned upside down. One man lamented the breakup of his marriage and the pain of the regret and guilt he felt for having caused it, while another man spoke of the extreme rejection he felt after his wife left him.

Many women were left in peril when their husband walked out. One lady shared how terribly alone and destitute she felt after her husband left, a situation which was further compounded by having to sell everything including most of the furniture in order to care for her two daughters. A number of women expressed similar feelings about being left with small children to look after with one saying she lost both her marriage and business and was left to raise three kids on her own.

Women typically suffered more than men from divorce and separation. One lady graphically described how she ended up in the psych ward after her husband left, was in and out for years after, and still suffers from depression. Similar but less severe was the lady whose husband of twenty-seven years left her, or the lady whose husband of over thirty years left suddenly to be with another woman but then returned after a time. The bitterness was palpable from a woman who recounted her husband leaving her at the age of fifty to be with his twenty-seven year old secretary.

In an era when it was often socially acceptable for men to be openly domineering over their wives physical abuse was a reality for many and often complicated further by mental, emotional and financial abuse. This was fueled by an environment where many women had few options and were often forced to be subservient to their husbands. One lady simply stated that she went from her father's house to her husband's house, while another expressed how her husband took advantage of her as a mother and housekeeper.

There were some graphic details including a mentally ill husband who a somber lady said "threatened to kill me," and the most poignant story from a lady with nine children whose gambling, alcoholic husband acted abusively and irresponsibly and left the family destitute. He would gamble away his pay and abuse the family in ways she wouldn't even say. This lady had been so extremely traumatized by her ex-husband, a man she hadn't been with or seen in decades, that when he died about ten years ago she said "I felt a great sense of relief just knowing he wasn't on this earth anymore."

"I felt a great sense of relief just knowing he wasn't on this earth anymore."

Family issues continued to come up as many people shared the difficulties of providing for a family. One lady simply said her most difficult time was "raising kids; they were monsters." Many people talked about problems related to the sheer number of children. One lady expressed that eight kids was just constant work, and several others said they had lots of kids and no money. A particularly touching story came from an impressive lady who exhibited no bitterness at having to support four children and a husband with long term illness on her salary as a meat wrapper.

Many women related how difficult it was to raise kids after death or separation like the previously mentioned lady whose alcoholic husband left the family of nine children destitute. She lamented that she couldn't give her children near what they needed much less what they wanted. One lady left an abusive relationship with four kids and went to welfare for help and another recounted the difficulties she faced looking after her family when her husband died at age forty-two leaving her with five teenagers at home. Another lady was unfortunate enough to be widowed twice with family to look after.

Other family issues that ranked as the most difficult things people ever had to deal with include a lady who was forced to go back to work when her baby was only two months old, and another lady whose teenage daughter ran away at fifteen never to be heard from again. There was never any word about her whereabouts and her body was never found. The outcome wasn't as bad for another a lady whose daughter ran away and eventually returned, but it was still a very difficult time and she said her daughter wasn't the same.

One lady related how her kids were into drugs and crime which created countless and ongoing problems for the family. She even raised her daughter's child for many years because of her own daughter's irresponsibility. Blended families also created difficulties for some as one man related how dealing with his step daughter, who he described as very bad, was amongst his most difficult trials.

Drug and alcohol abuse came up many times regarding the most difficult things people had to deal with. Spousal abuse was most common in relation to alcoholism, but there were also numerous stories of the pain of children being on drugs. Some of the previous stories of children dying were influenced by drugs and alcohol. It was extremely traumatic for parents to have children addicted to drugs as exemplified by a lady whose drug addicted daughter had her children permanently removed and adopted out. Her daughter continues on drugs, she hasn't seen her grandchildren for two years and said she has no visitation rights so most likely won't ever see them again.

There were also many personal stories of struggles with drugs and alcohol. One lady said she had suffered for many years with fear and anxiety that she tried to quell with alcohol, pot, and pills. A proud man said that the hardest thing for him was admitting he had a problem with alcohol because he always considered himself a very strong and together person. A similar response came from a man who said the toughest thing ever was "facing my alcoholism and getting my act together." Another man recounted how he spent four and a half months in rehab and has been sober for many years but almost drank when his wife died.

"Facing my alcoholism and getting my act together."

Depression and mental health issues created serious and difficult problems as several people spoke about their struggle with clinical depression. One unfortunate lady who suffered from bipolar disorder told how she was in and out of mental hospitals most of her life, survived numerous suicide attempts, lost friends, and was alienated from her family. Others openly questioned their emotional and mental well being with bouts of intense loneliness and self questioning. For others it was a spouse or loved one with mental illness that caused problems, like one lady who related the difficulties of living with a bipolar husband and another who described her husband as "schizophrenic and abusive."

Following the Great Depression it's not surprising that there were many stories about the difficulties of WWII. Several people went through the trauma of losing their father in WWII, and one lady's father was tortured in a Japanese slave labor camp. She knew of some of the horrors he endured and shared some with me, wincing as she spoke of her dad's description of witnessing the death of a thousand cuts. One lady's first husband was killed in WWII while other ladies were worried and alone as their husbands fought in Europe. One woman talked of working, looking after the kids and feeling lonely and depressed during the war years.

Almost twenty percent of the people interviewed were born in the UK and many had survived the London bombings, hearing the air raid sirens and sitting in shelters for hours. One lady remembered at the age of sixteen her friend's dad being killed by a bomb that hit the city. A cruel twist on a similar story came from another lady who told of how a family awaited the arrival of their dad on leave when the air raid sirens went off. The family was in the shelter when the dad returned and the house was bombed. The son was first up from the shelter and found his dead father.

One lady said that being in Germany during the war was the toughest time of her life, and another said that as a result of allied bombings she had several school friends killed. She also knew some Jewish people who were sent to camps. Another German lady said her father was killed during allied bombings and her town was flattened. A lady from Yugoslavia recounted how because her father was a union organizer some men in dark clothes came to their house late at night and took him away. The family never saw him again.

There were also many war stories recounted as their most difficult time from those who served in combat. A radio navigator who lost a brother during the war said he flew many bombing missions and feels very lucky to be alive. An infantryman shared how he was walking in a trench in Italy and saw something shiny on the ground. As he bent down to pick it up a sniper shot went over his head that certainly would have killed him.

Another man said he should have been killed on three different occasions and feels lucky just to be here. On one occasion he was in a group of nine soldiers when an enemy plane sprayed the ground with bullets and killed seven of them. Another time he was with his corporal in France and had run out of water. It was a mile back to the water truck and he lost the coin toss so had to make the hike. He returned to find his corporal dead. Third time lucky he was helping to clear a small town in France as the Germans retreated when fighting broke out. He stepped into a doorway that would only hold one person when another soldier came in. He offered the soldier the doorway and found another place for cover. When he returned the soldier was upright but as he touched him the soldier fell forward dead from a piece of shrapnel that had come through the door and entered his skull. This man truly felt lucky to be alive.

Other war related stories that were given as the most difficult times in life include a man who fought in the Korean War but wouldn't talk about what he did or saw. A sailor shared the trials and lifelong problems of being at Christmas Island in 1957 when seaman were subjected to the effects of a nuclear bomb for over a year. He said during a nuclear blast he held up his hands and could see his bones through the skin, but afterward his finger nails fell out and his hands suffered bleeding for many years. This was only the beginning of all the health problems with lumps, prostrate problems and many friends that have suffered and died from all manners of health problems since this terrible time. A more recent war story came from a person who served with the UN force in Rwanda and cited the indiscriminate killing and the stench of human bodies as one of his most difficult life experiences.

For many people childhood trauma ranked as the hardest times of their lives and it was surprising how people recounted vivid memories from so long ago as though they were fresh in their mind. It reminds us how impressionable children are and that everyone carries such trauma into their adulthood. Those who aren't able to come to grips with it suffer from it for life, but even those who are able to resolve it emotionally retain the vivid memories.

I asked a one hundred year old woman about the hardest thing she ever had to deal with and without hesitation the only response she gave was "being forced to do man's work on the farm as a child." She described herself as "dad's hard man" where she hurt her back and has suffered physical ailments for her entire life from the harsh conditions on the farm. More than one person spoke of the difficulty of farm work as a child and one lady said of her life "all of it has been hard, but working on the farm when I was a kid was the toughest, hauling water and milking cows. I did man's work as a female child." Another lady added that the girls not only had to work along with the men but then went inside and tended to the children and the household doing all the cooking and cleaning.

"All of it has been hard, but working on the farm when I was a kid was the toughest."

A surprising number of people lost a parent in their childhood, dad at age four, dad at age five, mom at age four, both parents at age twelve. For some the trauma of the event was trumped by the circumstances that followed including insecurity, emptiness, poverty or different living arrangements. One family suffered extreme poverty being raised without a father while another lady simply said she was starved as a child. At nine years old one lady lost her mom in the 1918 flu epidemic. Her mother suffered terribly crying for help and traumatizing the family with her pain before she died leaving only dad to care for five kids between the ages of six and thirteen. Another lady whose mom died when she was only nine was sent to live with a stern and strict aunt, the opposite to how her mother had been. Severe trauma came for another lady when at the age of ten her father was killed in an accident at work.

Several people who as children had lost a sibling ranked it as the most traumatic event of their lives. One lost a brother at age nine while another said her thirteen year old brother died when she was eighteen. Divorce and family break up for children also caused great hardship for some as they shared that their parent's divorce was the most traumatic time of their life, one at age five who felt terribly alone as an only child, another at age seven, and others as well.

Many people were candid in discussing the abuse they suffered at the hands of an alcoholic parent. One lady described her upbringing as "unpredictable with alcoholic parents" and said she has dealt with abandonment issues her whole life. Another simply said she had a "very difficult childhood with an abusive, alcoholic dad" while another said "my father was a drunk and I hated him for most of his life." One man was beaten so severely by his abusive father that it affected his eyesight. He left home and only saw his father once or twice after that. Another man at age twenty-one was arrested and spent ninety days in jail for beating up his alcoholic father. He said he had to put a stop to the years of abuse and mistreatment, especially toward his mother. This was echoed by several other people who suffered by witnessing their mother being abused. One lady said she was raised by "a very domineering father who mistreated my mother."

"My father was a drunk and I hated him for most of his life."

Other childhood trauma included a lady whose house burned down when she was twelve, a man who lost an arm in an accident, a lady who spent four years in hospital from fourteen to eighteen due to an illness, and a woman who had lockjaw at age fifteen.

A sad story came from a lady who said that as the eleventh of twelve children she was neglected by her parents and felt alone in a crowd of people. She added that she still feels that way. Another man said that one of the hardest times of his life happened when he was in grade five and his teacher told him he was the dumbest kid in the school. As a result he became very sensitive about being put down by people and has spent his life trying to prove he isn't stupid. He readily admits that at age sixty-nine he still carries it with him.

Perhaps the most bizarre story came from a lady who as a child in London during WWII survived the bombings. She and some friends found what they thought was a cow's eye and played with it, as children would, only to be traumatized later to find out it was the human eye from someone who had been killed in the bombing.

Another story of childhood trauma came from a lady I didn't even interview. I had done a speaking engagement for a group of seniors to share my story and solicit interviews. At the end as I was speaking with people and signing up interviewees a small intense lady waited until I was alone then walked up and said "I couldn't possibly do your interview. I have too much to hide" then quickly walked away. She paced around the room busying herself and once I was done with some others walked by without stopping and said "I was sexually abused as a child." It wasn't hard to figure out the most difficult part of her life and at about age seventy she had still not come to terms with it. This serves as a reminder that the emotional pain of childhood trauma lasts a lifetime if not dealt with.

"I couldn't possibly do your interview. I have too much to hide"

Being away from home proved most difficult for some people and one lady related her childhood anxiety from being raised in boarding schools. She didn't feel comfortable at the boarding school or when she returned home. Many people came from overseas and spoke of the anxiety of coming to a new country. One lady who was an only child felt terrible at leaving her mom in England because in her words "she had nothing else." Several others spoke of the difficulty adjusting to a new culture (and sometimes new language). One lady related a story of coming to Canada at the end of WWII to the land of opportunity and ended up struggling to survive on a remote Prairie farm. It was not at all what she expected and she felt terribly vulnerable and alone in a new country. There were similar stories from war brides.

For some people separation anxiety was caused by being conscripted into the army and taken away from home and family while for others it was a transfer at work. One man found it difficult to be away from home for extended periods of time for his work. One lady said that just moving all the time was most difficult not only for the work and expense of moving but lack of a home base. For one woman it was leaving her family home to go into a care home that was most traumatic. She misses her home and wishes she were still there.

Work related problems were paramount for some and created hardship for many families. A farming family lamented that they had eight crop failures in ten years and were forced to leave their farm with nothing. Another man shared how he was caught in what he vaguely described as a "no win" situation at work that resulted in him losing his job. This was compounded by the resulting financial problems for the family and the depression he felt personally.

A police officer spoke of the difficulty of working in major crimes and seeing the perpetrators and victims of abuse, sexual assault and other horrific crimes. A doctor spoke of the difficulty in seeing patients die simply saying "being a doctor was challenging." For a school superintendent the pressure he felt from the tremendous responsibility was the most difficult struggle of his life. One person working on a project in the jungles of Indonesia felt abandoned when her partner left to get married, and another man was terribly shaken when a man got killed in the plant where he worked.

"Being a doctor was challenging."

I have recounted and categorized many of the answers from asking people about the most difficult events and circumstances they've ever had to deal with, but the following responses either didn't have a category or struck me in some way that set them apart. The answers range from the almost comical to the bizarre.

When asked about her most difficult experience one lady said "nothing really bad ever happened to me. I've been really lucky," and another said "no problems or bad things happened to me. My parents were wealthy and my husband had a successful business so I've been a person of wealth my whole life." What a contrast from the tragedy in the preceding stories.

"Nothing really bad ever happened to me. I've been really lucky."

One person thought about it and had formulated an answer but didn't want to say so I didn't press him. Another man simply said "the unknown" is the hardest thing he's ever had to deal with. For one lady her most difficult challenge was "relationships, both male and female" and for another man it was as he put it "making friends, true close friends." One woman said the most difficult thing was to find a man to marry at age thirty-one. On a more comical note, the most difficult time for one man was giving his daughters the "birds and bees" talk. I thought at first he was joking but quickly realized he wasn't as he elaborated on how uncomfortable he was about it.

One man simply looked at me in a serious way and said "the hardest thing I've ever had to deal with is me, myself, thinking about things." For many of us the very toughest battle in life is the one inside our own head.

"The hardest thing I've ever had to deal with is me, myself, thinking about things."

A police officer said that the hardest thing he ever had to do was apprehend Doukabor children from their homes in the 1950s and 60s. It was difficult not only because he was separating children from their parents but because he had some personal misgivings about even doing it and was following orders that he didn't necessarily agree with.

One lady told me that the most difficult time in her life was when her husband created a scandal in the small town where they lived by stealing from the company he worked for. Everyone knew about it and the family had to leave the town in disgrace.

Two similar family issues involved parents and children in court proceedings. One lady was terribly upset about the fact that while still grieving the death of her husband her daughter took her to court over the family business. For another lady the most difficult time was testifying against her son (an only child) in a custody battle. They are still somewhat estranged.

An impressive Japanese-Canadian man recounted being evacuated to an internment camp during WWII. He was only eleven years old at the time and said the most difficult part of his life was seeing his parents lose their home, business and fishing boat. They never did fully recover from their losses after the war ended and they were freed. I then asked how he dealt with it personally and what he thinks looking back on it. His answer was surprising saying that the people of the town where the camp was were so kind to them that he actually had fun. People would give the children toys and presents and in some ways it was kind of a fun adventure.

Some people suffered cruel twists of fate like one lady who said the hardest time for her was finding out her second husband was a closet homosexual and another whose husband died on their daughter's twenty-first birthday. For another lady it was the number twenty-seven that she associated with hardship. In her words "we lost our second son in an accident at twenty-seven, one grandson committed suicide at twenty-seven, and another grandson was killed in an accident at twenty-seven."

I heard from a number of people who had compound tragedy and simply said that their "whole life" has been the hardest thing they've ever had to deal with. One lady endured the hardship of growing up on the Prairies in the 1930's. Her dad worked at two hard jobs, the farm and the coal mine. She suffered her whole life with heart problems from a heart defect and at sixteen her mom, who she described as her best friend, died. She married an unscrupulous man and contracted cervical cancer from a venereal disease he gave her. She was forced to support herself without a career, then after an unworkable reconciliation with her husband was left alone again. My impression was that she was more hurt than bitter, more tired than angry.

The most touching story and the one that had the most impact on me came from a lady who when asked about her most difficult times simply said "all of it." In her words "I've had a very, very hard life. My parents were terrible to me, my mother told me she hated me when I was five years old and even when I went to visit her on her death bed told me to get the hell out. I thought I was a boy until I was eleven years old when my brothers told me I wasn't. My mother provided for us, but there was no affection, patience or love."

CHAPTER 5

DID YOU HAVE A HAPPY LIFE?

GIVEN THE HEARTACHE recounted in the previous chapter, it is somewhat surprising that when asked if they had a happy life only three percent said no, seventeen percent said fifty-fifty, and an overwhelming eighty percent said yes. Some positive responses were a simple 'yes' with no comment while others were qualified with a vocal inflection or perhaps a comment on what they endured. Nevertheless, the responses were both genuine and encouraging. For every response to whether someone had a happy life I asked for reasons why in order to gain insights into what made people consider their life happy, unhappy or somewhere in between.

Three percent answered no and said that they didn't have a happy life. For most it was life circumstances that were so overwhelming they weren't able to control them or overcome them to the point where they could say life was good, or even satisfying. The trauma and heartache was such that no matter how things settled down later in life, they could never describe their life as happy.

One man shared that his youth was very tough and because of WWII didn't get properly set up in life. But more difficult for him was what he described as his lack of guts and the sadness he has felt his entire life from always being alone. For at least two people a lifetime of hard work, many and various jobs and lack of money has made life unhappy. One man cited the breakup of his marriage while one lady's life was made unhappy inside her marriage saying that she was bossed around all her life and never able to do the things she wanted to do.

For one lady the combination of a difficult childhood, marriage to an abusive and alcoholic husband then the heartache of seeing her kids mistreated prompted her to say she didn't have a happy life. This sentiment was echoed by a number of people who had suffered terribly through circumstances that can never be undone or forgotten. Due to an abusive, alcoholic husband and an unworkable family situation, one lady said that she has had a very hard life and feels terrible for having deprived her kids. Another person elaborated by saying "everything was very hard. I haven't seen my oldest daughter for twenty-five years because I was so bad to her. It was because of my own short comings from being starved as a child and dealing with my husband's illness." Another lady said life was unhappy because she suffered through a bad childhood, her parents split up, she worked very hard, her son died, she suffered through two divorces, then her third husband, with whom she was finally happy, got sick and died.

"Everything was very hard. I haven't seen my oldest daughter for twenty-five years because I was so bad to her."

Because of life difficulties and situations beyond their control seventeen percent of people interviewed couldn't bring themselves to say they had a happy life, but nor did they want to say it was unhappy so they settled on fifty-fifty. Many said life was tough early but better later, but most just qualified their response by pointing out the main reasons why they couldn't give an unqualified yes. One lady summed it up well by giving a list of reasons why she might be unhappy then said "it's been tough but I'm as happy as circumstances would allow."

"It's been tough but I'm as happy as circumstances would allow."

This was echoed by many people who spoke of tough times beginning at childhood. Over and over I heard the phrase "very tough childhood" and further examples such as "hard farm life on the Prairies," "poor parents," and "eight kids in a shack during the Depression." This was exacerbated for some by an abusive or alcoholic parent, a regimental and 'uppity' mom, and in one case the challenge of being raised by a blind mother.

The theme of hard work and lack of money continued into adult life as many people spoke of very tough times. One lady said with resignation "we were broke all the time and couldn't give the kids enough," while another talked about "poverty, illness and heartache." I heard from many who as children were raised in poverty but also from many who were adults during tough years like the Great Depression and suffered the hardship of trying to provide for their family with very few resources. Similar sentiments were summed up by one lady who simply said that overall she had "a very challenging life."

Following the Great Depression, WWII caused grief for many as several people spoke of tough times during the war years and one lady said "the war changed everything and changed my husband. He wasn't the same when he came back."

Not unexpectedly, relationship issues were a contributing factor to making life's happiness a fifty-fifty proposition. Some just spoke of "bad marriages" while others elaborated on alcoholism, abuse, divorce, and just general marital and family difficulties. This extended to other family members as a number of people spoke of estrangement from family.

Death was also a contributing factor as many people spoke of all the loved ones who were gone. One lady summed it up by saying "too many people have died on me," while another spoke of losing her husband, dad and mom. One man poignantly captured the sentiment by saying "tragedy has changed my values and what's most important. Money doesn't matter, my son died, my wife left, my brother was murdered and I've suffered many other family tragedies."

> *"Tragedy has changed my values and what's most important.*
> *Money doesn't matter, my son died, my wife left,*
> *my brother was murdered and*
> *I've suffered many other family tragedies."*

Death and related hardship created personal and emotional issues for many people, some of which remained unresolved. One lady said that she is emotionally unhappy while others spoke of being depressed, lonely, and "intense to a fault." A poignant description came from a lady who said that she has "a good defense mechanism and is able to stuff her feelings deep inside" while another said that because of a very tough childhood it took her a long time to "find herself" and now tries to make the best of every moment.

One particularly touching response came from a rather philosophical lady who said "I lost faith in God at a low point then saw a bumper sticker that said 'My God is not dead, sorry about yours.' I think you're born with a personality that makes you either happy or sad. I was born with an optimistic nature. Don't be a victim of circumstance. There are probably a string of crosses across the country saying '____ suffered here.'" Another lady simply said "once I got my life together it's been good."

"I think you're born with a personality that makes you either happy or sad."

Many of those who responded fifty-fifty also gave positive statements such as "life was difficult earlier but better later." Many just tried to see the positive in life as I again heard many statements about having a good outlook, making the best of things, maintaining a positive attitude, expecting the good, taking it as it comes, and maintaining a good sense of humor. More than a few people spoke of finding some happiness by establishing their own life and remaining thankful for it. One lady said that despite difficult circumstances happiness is something you can turn on, and another expressed the value of living in the present. Some talked about contrasts between difficulty and joy, hardship and satisfaction, while others spoke of good kids and a bad marriage, and many reiterated the sentiment that although life wasn't all they would have liked they still felt blessed in many ways.

TOP TEN REASONS FOR A HAPPY LIFE

- 1. Happy marriage
- 2. Kids and grandkids
- 3. Family and friends
- 4. Good Job and satisfying work
- 5. Just a naturally happy person
- 6. Good parents and happy childhood
- 7. Lucky
- 8. God / Faith / Church
- 9. Freedom to pursue life
- 10. Love people

The most popular reason from those who said they had a happy life was marriage. It's quite simple really. Marriage is intended to make our lives better so most people get married for companionship and to build a life with their partner. This was the case for most people. Yet even though it made many people's lives better it was also a source of great heartache for many others. Marriage, for better or worse, is the subject of the next chapter.

When asked why they had a happy life many people just included a reference to their spouse and left it at that. One woman simply said she just really enjoyed being married and having a family. Others made more specific comments like one man who said his life's joy came from being married to his wife. He described them as a childless couple who had a passionate admiration for one another for well over fifty years. One woman's happiness came from "getting married and getting away from the farm."

One couple had a special moment during the interview. They had both lost a spouse through death or divorce and have been together for maybe ten years, she in her early 80s and he in his late 70s. He was an understated but impressive man's man who had worked hard but maintained a gentle spirit. She gave various answers as to what made her happy, mostly to do with her upbringing and activities through her life. He then said his wife makes him happy. She stopped and looked at him rather taken back and there was a brief but revealing silence as she said "Well thank you _____, I've never heard you say that before." He blushed, she smiled, and the interview continued.

The second most popular response was children and grand children. One lady recounted the closeness of her family and how they did everything together, while another just smiled and said "I have great kids and grand kids." Eight children was the source of happiness for one lady, which is a positive response to what some considered onerous. A large family was both a blessing and burden, but most spoke of the happiness it brought despite the tough times they endured. Several people attributed their happiness to seeing their children doing well. One interesting comment came from a lady who said "it may sound strange, but I really like my kids." Of course she spoke of her adult children of whom she was proud and with whom she has become friends.

"It may sound strange, but I really like my kids."

A close third in popular responses was family and friends. Many people simply included family and good friends in the reasons their life was happy while others elaborated on how much those relationships have meant. One lady was descriptive saying of her family, they had kids so always had a purpose, enjoyed a simpler life, and were happy with less. They did the best they could and loved their family, kids and extended family. It was an ideal family network in many ways and created a happy life.

One person said he always got along well with people while another said "I like people and have lots of friends." One lady said her life was happy because of "God, family and friends" while others spoke of family ties, siblings and a close family. One lady summed it up by saying "we were all together, family, friends."

"I like people and have lots of friends."

The fourth most popular response was satisfying work. As previously pointed out, work consumes a substantial part of our lives and to some extent shapes who we are so it's not surprising that it would factor in to whether or not someone had a happy life. Most people found contentment in a job where they could support their family and feel like they were making a difference to society, but because this was explored in the work question, most people just referred to a "satisfying job" as part of a happy life.

The next most popular response was curious given all the difficult circumstances people endured, but it seems many people feel that happiness is largely determined by a combination of heredity and attitude. One lady put it succinctly by attributing her happiness to heredity saying that her mom was a naturally happy person while another said her disposition is such that she has a smile for everybody. A fairly typical response from likeminded people was "I'm just a happy person; I just see things in a positive way." Many people said that despite the ups and downs in life they didn't worry too much about things or get depressed in the face of difficulty but just naturally see the bright side of any situation. More than one person just said "I'm happy go lucky."

"I'm just a happy person; I just see things in a positive way."

Similar to those who felt a natural bent to be happy others suggested it was more of a choice and attitude. Many people made statements like "I decided to be happy," "life is what you make it," and "it has to do with your attitude." Similar comments include "I don't believe in the negative," "I laugh a lot and have a positive attitude," and "I grew up poor but always tried to make the best of it." Such sentiments were summed up by the old adage repeated by several people "I always look for a silver lining." These responses were remarkable considering I had just asked people about the hardest things they had to deal with only to hear a litany of tragic stories. Then the next question was whether they had a happy life and I heard many examples of overcoming difficulty and finding a way to stay positive about life.

"I grew up poor but always tried to make the best of it."

Some responses were quite forceful as one lady put it "we have a choice to be happy or sad. I choose to be happy. Nothing is so bad that you can't find something happy." Similar comments include "I planned to be happy," "despite the problems, I have always done what I needed to do and have overcome things," and "don't worry; be happy." This thinking promotes the philosophy many people reiterated that despite your circumstances "life is what you make it." One lady's recipe for happiness was to say "I'm a happy go lucky person and look at the bright side. My dad used to say that if you have an issue dwell on it for ten minutes then move on."

"We have a choice to be happy or sad. I choose to be happy."

There is no doubt that parents and upbringing have a tremendous influence on children, both good and bad, and many people attributed much of their happiness to loving parents and a good upbringing. They spoke of their parent's struggle to provide for the family and the love conveyed in the process. Such circumstances created a lifetime love and respect for parents that was palpable as one person said with a warm smile "my mother was an angel" and another lady spoke of "a very good dad." The start of a happy life for many people began with what they described as "my loving parents" and "fantastic parents."

"My mother was an angel"

Many people attributed their life happiness to luck. Having looked around and seen tremendous heartache and struggle, some people just felt lucky to have had the life they lived. One person acknowledged she had a lot to be thankful for while another spoke of a "charmed existence" and added "love is the greatest thing." Several people made comments like "I've been fortunate," "I've been very lucky all my life," and "things just worked out for me." One lady summed it up by saying "everything has been as good as I expected, or better."

"Everything has been as good as I expected, or better."

Further responses to those things that made life happy were fairly typical as some people spoke of their faith in God bringing great joy to their lives while others talked about the freedom they enjoyed to do what they wanted. One enthusiastic man said "I do the things that I like," while one lady said she always had a little money to do the things she wanted and another just said "laughter; I've done everything I wanted to do."

A number of people attributed their overall love for others as key to life's happiness. One lady's philosophy was as simple as "I'm outgoing and I love people," and a large, jolly man impressed me by his simple philosophy "I love people and people love me." By the way he carried himself I could see he lived what he said.

"I love people and people love me."

Some people mentioned things like good health, sports and various other activities that contributed to a happy life. And of course a good sense of humor carried many people through life's trials. One man said that because he was raised in an orphanage he learned to appreciate things at an early age.

Acceptance was the key to happiness for some people. Many just said they "take life as it comes" and try to make the best of it. One lady said that even though she grew up poor, they accepted their situation and enjoyed it the best they could.

Some of the more curious or quirky answers were quite funny. When asked if she had a happy life one lady grinned and said "yes, I was a little bugger." A somewhat uppity woman gave an unqualified 'yes' and was happy to have lived a charmed life of wealth. Then she leaned across the table and said "I don't know if you can tell or not, but I was VERY attractive when I was younger." I smiled. Conversely, one lady said that happiness came from being considerate of others and always remembering to spell 'self' with a small 's.'

The pragmatic approach was the key for some people as one woman had a simple philosophy saying "I've made my life happy by getting rid of the unhappiness," and another elaborated saying "I'm happy just being alive. I just keep going. If bad things happen I just carry on. I'm a fatalist, Que sera sera." This sentiment was echoed by a person who simply said "I love life."

"I've made my life happy by getting rid of the unhappiness"

One well educated man laughed condescendingly at being asked if he had a happy life and responded by asking "What kind of question is that?" Then he answered yes, saying that for him happiness comes from "just being alive, having good health, and always having what I needed. I lived my life, did well at my job, and helped the kids I taught."

Two people qualified their answer by saying they didn't have a 'happy' life but had a 'good' life. This was curious to me as I pondered the distinction. One person didn't elaborate, as though I would know what she meant. But the other lady elaborated somewhat by saying "no, not happy but good: Good marriage, good kids, good mom, schooling, and teaching." In retrospect I should have questioned her further but what I think she meant is that her life wasn't happy in the sense of being fun or easy, but it worked out. She did what she had to do and was satisfied with her effort and the result. It was workable and successful but it wasn't something she could describe as happy, only good.

CHAPTER 6

MARRIAGE

WHAT'S THE SECRET to a long and happy marriage? That's the question I sought to answer from those who achieved success and longevity in marriage. Is it just a lot of work and compromise or are some couples just made for each other? Is it a combination of work and compatibility? And how do people define a long and happy marriage? Is it a love affair, a functional partnership, something in between or something else all together?

Some couples described their marriage as a functional partnership, a lifelong arrangement for mutual benefit, while some others said their marriage started out as a love affair and evolved into a functional partnership. For a few couples the love affair was still evident as one couple in their eighties batted their eyes and smiled affectionately at one another while we spoke. It's part of the mystery of marriage.

Of the over three hundred people interviewed, seventy-four percent had been married only once. This does not disparage those who were married more than once because many breakups were due to various factors that will be discussed shortly. But it was those who managed to sustain a single long term and happy relationship that had the most light to shed on the subject. Of those married only once, eighty-three percent said they were happily married while seven percent said they were not and ten percent said it was fifty-fifty.

TOP TEN REASONS GIVEN FOR LONG AND HAPPY FIRST MARRIAGE

▌ 1. Compatibility
▌ 2. Loving each other / caring / considerate
▌ 3. Being friends / having fun / doing stuff together
▌ 4. Working together to build a life
▌ 5. Seeing your partner as a good person

6. Working at it to get along / Communication
7. One or both being laid back or happy go lucky
8. Kids / family / home
9. Trust / Mutual respect
10. Faith

The answers given were loosely and somewhat arbitrarily categorized to reflect particular reasons for success and longevity in marriage. The top answer from those who were happily married was compatibility. It seems rather obvious, but compatibility over a long term relationship is much different than a perceived compatibility in shorter term relationships. The long term compatibility people spoke of includes common perspective, similar values, similar interests, a similar outlook on life, and similar preferences. Such relationships were described by many as "a good match," "a real connection," and "the right person for me." For some it was chemistry while others said they found their soul mate, the person they were meant to be with.

Others didn't like the idea of soul mates but acknowledged a deep connection with their spouse. Some simply said they "just clicked" and "got along well" while one person said "we were very compatible and found happiness with each other." Speaking of their compatibility one lady said "my husband adored me and it was mutual." Compatibility for another lady meant he was quiet and she was noisy. She added that he was a gentleman which was perhaps telling of what he lovingly endured.

"We were very compatible and found happiness with each other."

A more profound answer came from a lady who said that while they did have similar interests the key to their longevity and happiness was that they managed to stay in love. Many couples may start out in passionate love and end up in a partnership, but for others love grows and matures. "I couldn't imagine it any better" is what one lady said in front of her husband. "We supported each other. I gave one hundred percent. We were very compatible. I wrote a list of things we saw the same and had over thirty."

"I couldn't imagine it any better."

The next most popular response had to do with affectionate love and acting in a caring and considerate way toward one another. For some it was as simple as saying that through all the years they "were very considerate of each other," "were always there for each other," and "were affectionate and nice to each other." Such couples shared each other's concerns and recognized each other's needs. One lady said "he never yelled at me and we were kind to each other." For others it was the reassurance in their voice as they said things like "he loved me," "I loved him dearly," or "he spoiled me."

One man spoke affectionately about how his wife put up with him and was understanding as he was away a lot for work. A widower lovingly said marriage is "give and take. I was very passionately in love with her and never met anyone like her so I never re-married." And a widow said of her husband that "he was very caring and understanding" and added "never let the sun go down on your anger."

"I was very passionately in love with her and never met anyone like her, so I never re-married."

The third most popular response had to do with being friends and enjoying each other's company. As one lady put it, "my goal was to find a companion that was my greatest friend. It was a good partnership and we got along well. We solved problems together." There were many responses like "we're exceptionally good friends" and "he was my best friend."

Friendship was closely associated with companionship as many spoke of getting along well and having lots of fun together. Many people reflected on good times and what wonderful company they made for one another as they shared everything together. One lady spoke of her husband's likeable personality while another said her husband was "just a heck of a nice guy." A good description of contentment came from a lady who said her husband was very tolerant and uncomplicated and therefore easy to be around with few problems in the marriage.

But clearly being best friends is not enough for marriage if there is to be romance and passion. In fact some would suggest that focusing too much on friendship can undermine romance and passion. This was addressed by one lady who found a balance and said "I liked him as a person and loved him too," and another lady who said "for fifty years we are best friends, do lots together and enjoy each other's company. We put each other first, even over the kids."

"We put each other first, even over the kids."

Closely related to mutual friendship is the notion of working together to build a life which was for many a key element to a long and successful marriage. Some described their marriage in almost clinical terms as a life partnership in which their relationship was largely defined by work and success in maintaining a home and raising kids. But most people just spoke of the loving struggle that brought them closer and built their relationship as they worked hard to achieve common goals. One couple in their nineties spoke lovingly of how they worked hard together for over seventy years, and others spoke with pride of working hard together for many years to sustain themselves, maintain a home and raise their family.

According to twenty percent of those happily married, seeing their spouse as a good person that they respected led to longevity and long term marital satisfaction. Many wives spoke of the good person they married using phrases like "he was a wonderful man," "he was a good man, good provider and good with the kids," "he was a very thoughtful and good man," and "he was a kind and good person." One lady simply smiled and said "I picked a good guy."

Men were even more glowing about their wives using descriptions like "she was a great woman," "she was an excellent person," and "I married the right woman." Some offered more detail saying things like "she was an exceptional person who knew herself very well," and "she was wonder woman and did everything, kids, home, and never complained." One man said that he had a "good wife" then added "I married a good person, better than me," and another said his long and happy marriage was due to his "incredible wife" saying "I trust her and love her, and we are committed to one another for life."

"I married a good person, better than me."

I asked many people whether long and happy marriages are more a result of compatibility or working at it. The consensus was that compatibility helps but it still takes work, and more for some than others. Many people who said that their marriage was happy also said they both had to work at it. One man summed up this sentiment saying "despite arguments we worked it out. We were compatible but we worked at it."

"Despite arguments we worked it out. We were compatible but we worked at it."

Many people spoke generally of "ups and downs" but some were more specific admitting that "we weathered the tough times and compromised," "we learned to work together through disagreements," and "it was hard work but we're from the old school so we just worked it out." Another said "we worked on each other. Divorce is not an option so we work it out. If you care for someone you don't want to hurt them." Many people reiterated this sentiment and one man rather crudely said "she was my wife for life. I claimed her when I saw her," while another said "don't give up. You have to work at it. Divorce wasn't heard of which allowed me to grow inside my marriage." It was an insightful perspective and testimony from such people who saw finality to being committed to one person despite the inevitable struggles.

For many people 'working at it' meant both parties being willing to give and take, make adjustments, be tolerant of the other, and be able to talk. The subject of communication came up many times as people spoke of "talking things through" and "not suppressing or burying anger." "We talked about things and I supported my husband," "we were very different in personality but you just have to get through things and can't be selfish," and "we worked it into a partnership in which we were both empowered."

"We worked it into a partnership in which we were both empowered."

Long term and successful marriages seem more elusive for many in today's world so it provides great insight when someone elaborates on the effort involved in making it work. Several people offered more in depth explanations like one man who said "I have a tolerant wife. She loves me and I love her, permanently. We are very different but it works; communication is the key. Listen."

An insightful woman said that the key is "real communication" explaining that "sometimes people talk but don't communicate. The other person has a different view and that's okay. Don't give up easily and accept that you can't change people." But then she admitted "I wasn't looking for marriage and don't believe in soul mates," which gave her analysis even more credibility in an odd sort of way.

"Sometimes people talk but don't communicate."

A widow who said she was happily married for many years offered an analysis that was not sugar coated saying "we stuck it out when things were tough. You can fall in love two or three times with the same person. I loved him or hated him but he was a good man, so mostly I loved him even though we almost split up over his drinking." And another honest widow said "we had lots of tiffs, give and take. Is it passion or partnership? It starts out passionate and becomes a partnership. Concentrate on the quality of your marriage rather than striving for too much material stuff."

"I loved him or hated him but he was a good man,
so mostly I loved him."

Some people attributed longevity in marriage to a happy go lucky or laid back spouse. One lady said her husband "was very laid back," while another described her husband as "mellow," and another said her husband was the "best half and very easy going." Women seemed to appreciate a husband with a good disposition who was easy going. One lady rather comically said "we didn't fight at all. He wouldn't argue." Men also appreciated an easy going spouse as one man described his wife with a "good disposition" and another spoke of the joy of "being married to a happy person who has a good outlook on life."

For many people family, children and a fulfilling home life were an integral part of a long and happy marriage and there were many comments like "we were very family oriented," "I just wanted to have a family," and "it was true love and we did everything as a family." This was reiterated by one man who when asked why he was happily married said they "got along well, had three kids and did a lot of camping." Another man lovingly said it was "my wife's devotion to the family and me."

"It was true love and we did everything as a family."

Trust and respect for one another also came up frequently as many people said their marriage lasted largely due to the respect they had for one another. One person attributed it to "love and mutual respect," while another woman said her husband garnered a lot of respect because "we trusted each other and he was good to my mother." But it wasn't without some irony as there were several comments like "we had mutual respect. She put up with a lot," and "we had mutual respect. Sometimes we would fight and not talk for days, but we enjoyed each other's company."

"Sometimes we would fight and not talk for days, but we enjoyed each other's company."

One woman described her excellent husband as "very capable," and another said rather clinically "we respected each other, and made decisions together. I married the right person." One man reiterated this sentiment saying of his wife "I respected her. I found the right person." The idea of commitment and mutual respect was best captured by the lady who said "first you SAY your wedding vows, and then you need to LIVE them."

"First you SAY your wedding vows, and then you need to LIVE them."

Faith and religion played a role for some as there were those who simply cited "religion" as contributing to the success and longevity of their marriage while others spoke of church involvement having a positive influence on marriage and family. For one couple it was "fifty-nine years of faith and church involvement." Of her long and successful marriage one lady lovingly said it greatly helped "having the Lord in our lives."

For others it was humor that really helped carry their marriage through rough patches and make the good times better. Many people referred to their spouse's "good sense of humor" and one man laughingly said of his marriage "it drives me crazy sometimes, but we have good sense of humor and are compatible."

"It drives me crazy sometimes, but we have good sense of humor and are compatible."

Freedom and independence within marriage were important for many people, especially for some women from this era who were often expected to be subservient to their husband. It was important for one lady that she was allowed to speak her mind, and she felt empowered because her husband trusted her to look after the family money. Another woman simply said "he let me be who I wanted to be."

But ironically the issue of freedom wasn't always as positive as one might think. One man reservedly said "I had a wife that put up with me. I was away a lot for work and she understood. She gave me lots of freedom." In a matter of fact way one lady said of her marriage "we were independent," and another spoke of her successful and happy marriage but added "we each minded our own business."

"We each minded our own business."

There were many such people who said they were happily married for many years but qualified their answer. Examples include a lady who said she did have a happy marriage but added that her husband had psychological damage from the war, or another lady who said of their marriage "there were lots of ups and downs but it was okay." It was hardly a ringing endorsement of their marriage but she insisted they were happy. And one lady felt it worth mentioning that it was very important to her that her husband was a very clean person.

One man said of his marriage "we're very different but complementary. She's affectionate and more carefree. We're very comfortable with each other." This was more the idea that opposites attract, a compatibility found in differences, which is perhaps true if one is laid back and the other more outspoken. But this was the exception not the rule in this study as most happily married couples spoke of their similarities rather than differences, and in many respects opposites more often repelled than attracted.

Several women spoke of being spoiled or treated like a princess by their husband. One lady went so far as to say "everything was my way. My husband thought so much of me we never had a single argument." Another woman was thankful for her husband's helpful ways and attributed their long and happy marriage to his willingness to garden, cook, clean and Hoover. "He did most of the Hoovering and was very helpful."

"Everything was my way. My husband thought so much of me we never had a single argument."

Several wives were tolerant of their husband's self indulgences, something many husbands appreciated at the time and regretted somewhat looking back. One man simply said "we've never really had a fight. She's been silent at times. I drank and she put up with me," and another said that his marriage lasted but admitted that he "stopped at the bar too often and spent too much time at the Legion."

Some answers were almost contradictory such as the self described happily married woman who said "he took care of me and was devoted to me. He was prince charming and a good provider" then added, "but he was a very controlling husband, controlled all the money and every aspect of our lives. I knew my place." There were many such examples of people who said they were happily married then recounted something seemingly contrary.

A surprising number of people claimed they were happily married, many for ten years or more, then explained how their relationship dissolved. One man said his wife just didn't like military life so went back to her hometown, and another said he was on the road driving so much that his wife eventually left when he was away. This same sentiment was recounted by a woman who said she was happily married but then said "we weren't together much so we separated. He was away nine out of ten years." One man offered no explanation other than nonchalantly saying "my ex and I are still good friends. We parted on good terms." Another man said he was happily married to his first wife but explained "we were married for twenty-six years but we drifted apart. I was away too much. She was wealthy and I wasn't. Eventually I was in to cars too much and other stuff. We never even said goodbye. It just dissolved."

"My ex and I are still good friends. We parted on good terms."

Several people admitted the demise of their first marriage from affairs they had while others said they were happy but their partner was not, saying things like "he left for another woman," "he had a mistress and a child," and "I was happy but she left me for someone else." One man loved his wife and was willing to stay with her but said "she was attracted to other men" so it was unworkable. One lady loved her husband and said he was a good man "but he wanted to party seven days a week. You can't raise a family."

Many people whose first marriage managed to stay together for more than ten years rated their level of happiness at fifty-fifty. There were many reasons for this beginning with those who conceded they got married too young and things didn't work out as they had hoped. For one woman it started by reluctantly moving away from her hometown and family. One man spoke fondly of his wife and how they worked together and had lots of fun but added that her emotional baggage from a dysfunctional upbringing really depleted their marital satisfaction. Another man said of his first marriage that it was good at first but admitted he was young and naïve while she was controlling. One lady provided a vivid description of her first marriage saying "I was married at twenty, we were always short of money, and he was a socialite and I wasn't. He got very involved in union work then left me after ten years."

Getting married because of pregnancy was mentioned a few times and one person said "we fell out of love. She was pregnant when we got married and I shouldn't have married her." Another said of her marriage "he didn't love me when we married. I asked him why he married me and he said I was a good kid."

"We fell out of love. She was pregnant when we got married and I shouldn't have married her."

Not surprisingly alcohol had a detrimental effect on many marriages as people readily admitted things like "I was really busy and a drunk," or "I was a drunk and I left." One man said his wife drank too much while one woman said of her husband "he was wild and drank a lot."

"He was wild and drank a lot."

Another lady said she was happily married at first but then he became possessive and the children didn't like their dad because he was cantankerous. This was echoed by another lady who said "he worked hard and I looked after the family. We worked it out. He was a good provider but he was stern and strict."

Some fifty-fifty marriages weren't necessarily unhappy just fraught with indifference. One woman said that her husband was a good man but rated their marriage as fifty-fifty without saying why. A similar sentiment came from another lady who said they had the same interests and outlook but rated the marriage at fifty-fifty without elaborating. Another said with resolve "you just do the best you can." A more specific description came from a lady who spoke of a "very passive husband" saying "there have been ups and downs (work problems and money problems) but he loves me and has been very steady. We have a functional partnership."

"You just do the best you can."

Incompatibility was a critical issue for many people as one woman married almost fifty years said with resolve "we are very different people," and a man said of his first marriage "we grew apart after a while. I met another woman and left her."

"We grew apart after a while. I met another woman and left her."

Perhaps the most contradictory answer came from a woman who said "I met my soul mate, but it was a stormy marriage. He was very demanding but we had lots of fun together." A similar answer came from a man who said "I'm laid back and she's outspoken. We have our differences." One lady complained "he always had to be busy and too involved. We were interested in same things and had similar political views. He was away a lot; we loved each other." Another lady simply said "I long for peace and fewer battles, less argument and more discussion."

"I long for peace and fewer battles, less argument and more discussion."

Several people spoke of how sickness lowered marital satisfaction as one lady said they have nice children but had ups and downs in their marriage and she's been sick for many years. A similar story came from another lady who spoke of being happy farming together but her husband's illness took its toll on their relationship.

Some fifty-fifty first marriages survived while others did not. One widow who stuck it out for many years said "I was stubborn and stuck to my commitment; he had many kids from a previous marriage which was challenging and he didn't discipline the kids much. He was also manic and too philosophical so we had more of a functional partnership than a love affair." Another woman said they were compatible and had twenty wonderful years but later he turned to alcohol and cigarettes and died of cancer of the esophagus and a blood clot; he abused his body and thought I was a nag."

Surprisingly some marriages sounded like complete failures yet were still rated as fifty-fifty. One lady shared, "I was homesick and he was German. He was nice at times but a womanizer who had a girlfriend. I finally left but stuck it out for years. I was patient but he would stay out for days. He said 'I can do whatever I want and no one wants you with four kids.' He forged my signature and cashed in our life insurance." An equally awkward circumstance was described by a somewhat cynical man who said "I got married because it was the thing to do and it was somewhat of a functional partnership. We were both career oriented and we still live together but just as friends. I could have just not bothered getting married and it would have been better."

I could have just not bothered getting married and it would have been better."

It's hard to imagine that there could be worse marital circumstances but of everyone interviewed, including all those married more than once, over sixteen percent of those interviewed gave an unequivocal "no" when asked if their first marriage was happy. There was the typical litany of reasons from incompatibility to immaturity but by far the most common reason was alcohol and the inevitable physical, mental, emotional and financial abuse they suffered.

Many people simply attributed the demise of their first marriage to alcohol while others were more specific. One lady admitted "I was an alcoholic and destroyed my marriages by drinking and arguing." But it was predominantly men who were the heavy drinkers, and physical abuse almost always accompanied alcohol abuse. Many women simply said they were married to an "abusive alcoholic."

"I was an alcoholic and destroyed my marriages by drinking and arguing."

Alcohol was often accompanied by other vices as one lady described her husband as a "drunk and a womanizer" while another candidly admitted her husband "had all the vices and another woman." Another said of her husband "he was like Jekyll and Hyde, a heavy drinker and abusive." Some people were unaware of the potential problems as one lady said she didn't know her husband well enough when they married and he turned out to be an alcoholic. Some had it even worse as one lady admitted her husband was "terribly abusive, drinking, gambling and moving all the time."

"He was like Jekyll and Hyde, a heavy drinker and abusive."

Many first marriages broke up from one partner leaving to be with someone else. "He fell in love with someone else and left" is what one woman said while another said her husband left to be with her best friend. She then said reflectively "I was more hurt by my friend. I don't think he loved me." A similar story came from a man whose wife of seventeen years had suffered from chronic depression and ran off with his best friend. But then he grinned and said "he did me a favor." The pain was much greater for another family as one woman said "he was a womanizer who was never happy with just me. One son told me to leave but I had nowhere to go. He eventually left me for another woman."

Many people said their marriage failed largely due to incompatibility saying it was a "bad match" or they were "not compatible at all." One lady simply said they were incompatible, that her husband was "a good provider but too uptight and critical."

Incompatibility took many forms but disagreement over the desire to have children was mentioned by many people as a primary factor in the demise of their marriage. One woman said "he didn't want kids and was threatening to me," and a man said "she didn't want kids so we grew apart and were incompatible." One man said his wife wanted kids but he didn't and suggested that she only married him for money and spent lots of it so the relationship ended.

Another form of incompatibility was immaturity as many people spoke candidly about the mistake it was to get married so young. One lady said they were simply too young and didn't grow together while another chalked it up to immaturity saying "I was very naïve." Another woman said of her husband "he was very immature, didn't appreciate home life and cheated on me." One man said his marriage lasted a very short time and admitted he never wanted to marry her. Perhaps the most vivid description came from a lady who said "I was married at eighteen. He was bipolar, moody and up-tight. There was no affection and he didn't touch me for over a year."

"I was very naïve."

It's difficult to hear all the sad stories of how marriages failed and about the people who suffered in the process, but perhaps it can teach us something about expectations verses reality and making decisions based on what we would like to happen rather than what is likely to happen. For one unfortunate lady she suffered from virtually every problem. "He was very self centered and did what he wanted. He stepped out many times and drank too much. He left eventually after forty-three years. He was a terrible father and husband."

Many other women suffered at the hands of abusive men as one lady spoke of her husband's stubbornness saying "I left him. He was very cold and wouldn't talk to me for up to three weeks. He spent lots of money on his hobbies; he was outwardly a great guy but once the door closed it was different." Another lady said her first marriage became "an endurance test. He was a good person, but it was dissatisfying for both. He didn't mature. We were like strangers. He came home from the war a different person, didn't work much, and golfed a lot."

Several people willingly admitted that they caused the breakup of their first marriage including a lady who said "I was domineering, dependant, jealous and was set to destroy it due to abusive parents," and one man who frankly admitted "I worked too much and was a male chauvinist." It was the opposite problem for one lady who said her husband didn't work enough and another who said her husband went crazy and was taken away. Several women were extremely disappointed in their first husband for family issues. One woman said that her mother in law was too imposing while another said her husband didn't help with her old parents and didn't care if their girls got educated.

"I was domineering, dependant, jealous and was set to destroy it due to abusive parents."

Many people said their first marriage was unhappy and offered no explanation. Some were even still unhappily married. One lady simply said it was too personal to say why she was unhappy and offered no more information. But it's important to keep in mind that like those who managed to stay together, many of these people also didn't believe in divorce but had little or no choice explaining that it's only possible to work it out if both parties are in some way willing or if one party is willing to accept a life time of abuse and disappointment. From the stories recounted here it's clear that some marriages were simply doomed to fail regardless of how much one spouse tried to hold on.

"I worked too much and was a male chauvinist."

The most poignant story about the demise of a marriage came from a lady who said that as a teenager her first husband was a man who had hung around the family farm and "raped me but nothing happened to him." She added "eventually I married him then he walked out after nineteen years." Then after a failed second marriage she re-married her first husband saying "we re-married then he died of cancer. I pitied him. I was a man-slave and dominated because of my childhood pattern."

Many of those married more than once did so because of the death of their first spouse. One lady had the misfortune of having three husbands die for various reasons, and for another it was twice. One man was very happy with his second wife and operated a successful business with her but she died of cancer. A similar story came from a man who said that his second wife was much more compatible than his first and in his words was "game to do things" but she also died an early death.

For those who were divorced most had intended to be married only once and were disappointed with the breakup of their first marriage. Of course many of the same problems occurred for those in their second marriage but fortunately for some they were more discerning and felt that they got it right on their second time and managed to remain married for life. Yet statistically the numbers weren't as good for happiness in their second marriage as only fifty-nine percent said they were happily married, down from eighty-three percent of those married only once. Fifteen percent said it was fifty-fifty, up from ten percent for those married only once, and the remaining twenty-six percent said they were not happily married, up from seven percent of those married only once.

Of those who said they were happily married the second time around many people offered general references to being more compatible, being friends, having similar interests and outlooks and having lots in common. One lady spoke of how she met a wonderful man and knew right away he was the one. Another said of her second husband that he wasn't an alcoholic like her first husband and they were able to enjoy many things together. For her, and some others, compatibility also included acceptance of step children and extended family.

Compatibility had various definitions and for some it meant independence. Several people made comments like "we have our own interests," "we are independent and have enough money to do what we want," and "she was tolerant of my long work hours." But for most it meant a close and deep connection as one lady said "we appreciated each other and the type of people we were. We had both been married before to the wrong people," and another lady said that they had the "same interests and stayed in love." One woman smiled as she spoke of her second husband saying "he was eighteen years older than me. We had the same principles, kind, gentle, caring, and I felt adored by him."

"We appreciated each other and the type of people we were. We had both been married before to the wrong people."

There were some very touching descriptions of fulfilling second marriages like one man who said "we were very happy, very compatible; we fell in like long before we fell in love," and another man who said of his second wife she was a "good woman, very practical, beautiful, loving, and very capable." Another man boasted of his second wife saying "she was a positive influence on the family, honest, good morals, and a hard worker for thirty-three years," while another said "I respect her; she's my best friend."

"We fell in like long before we fell in love."

Many people offered insights in to what they had learned from being married more than once like one lady who found it important that "he treated me like a person and I was important to him." One man offered that "you have to laugh; be realistic." For one lady consideration was the key to her long term successful and happy second marriage. And perhaps the best insight came from a lady who explained the difference between boyfriends and husbands saying that "boyfriends don't like responsibility. Some people are married to their boyfriend."

"Boyfriends don't like responsibility.
Some people are married to their boyfriend."

For all the successful second marriages the statistics and stories reveal that they were in many ways just as difficult for some as their first, and there were many people who did not find the marital satisfaction they were looking for describing their second marriage as fifty-fifty. Comments include "we were happy at times then grew apart," and "I'm still dealing with demons and we have problems."

"I'm still dealing with demons and we have problems."

One man said his marriage was happy "to a point, but not perfect. We took out a marriage contract and have lots of freedom. We do our own thing and we respect each other." From a woman who was happily married the first time and only fifty-fifty the second she said "it's not the same, not a love affair and I'm not as in love as I was. But he's a good man. I'm content." A rather philosophical man who rated his second marriage at fifty-fifty simply said that "successful relationships need humor and flexibility."

"Successful relationships need humor and flexibility."

For those who said their second marriage was not happy, alcohol and related problems were once again the most frequent responses. The references to "abusive alcoholic" came up many times as some people went from one abusive relationship to another speaking of "drunken, gambling womanizers." One lady admitted to her own alcoholism and the destruction of her own marriage, as did another woman who was set to destroy her second marriage as she had her first. One man admitted his mistake in marrying his widow's friend who he said "smoked and drank and died of lung cancer."

Some used descriptions like "controller" to describe their second spouse while one lady said her second husband was "jealous and mentally ill." This was similar to another situation in which a lady said her husband suffered mental illness. One lady said of her second marriage "we were too far apart. I was a city girl and he was a country boy. I just chose the wrong person," and another lady described the embarrassment she suffered when her second husband committed fraud and stole money from his company describing him as "money focused."

The biggest mistake was admitted by one woman who said of her second husband "he didn't like my boys and sexually abused my girls. It was a complete mistake and never should have happened. He had no job. He was a handyman." Several other people were candid in admitting the mistake they made marrying for the second time like one man who said "it was a rebound relationship and she had two kids. The mixed family didn't work and I wasn't the dad." Another man admitted his shortcomings saying of his second marriage "it was a flash in the pan, a big mistake. She was beautiful but we were incompatible. I was vain and self centered."

"It was a flash in the pan, a big mistake."

Again there was a lady who said of the breakup of her second marriage that it was too personal to share, and another woman who had followed a lifelong pattern of dysfunction and abuse said "there was a lack of communication. I learned how to fish and worked in his business but never got paid. He left me and we got divorced."

There was a real sense from those who had been through two mediocre or failed marriages that they weren't going to find fulfilling long term love, and unfortunately for some it was true. But for those who were married three and four times there were a few that found some happiness despite the scars they bore.

Some people were third time lucky as one person was happy to say she has been married to her third husband for forty years. Another said they have a good partnership and she finally met a good man with good principles who is interesting, active, shows mutual respect and shares the same values. Two people finally found some measure of happiness on their fourth marriage, one whose husband didn't cheat as the three previous had, and one who finally married a man who wasn't an abusive alcoholic.

One man whose previous wife had died of cancer said of his happy third marriage "we have a daughter together, a business, and are very compatible. I respect her very much." Another man was happy because she was a good woman, they were compatible and there were no children to deal with. Then there was the woman whose two previous husbands had died and her third husband died after eleven months of marriage. She was happily married three times and remains a widow.

Not surprisingly there were those who were unlucky at love for their entire life. Of those married three or four times some described them as fifty-fifty. For some it was just accepting that this is as good as it gets and were happy to have a peaceful and workable relationship. One lady who had been married three times previously and was abandoned by her fourth husband still described her marriage as fifty-fifty even though "he drank too much, travelled lots as trucker and he left me when I got sick saying 'All I ever wanted was for you to be healthy.'" Then she smiled and sarcastically said "most people take their garbage out to the road; I married my garbage."

"Most people take their garbage out to the road; I married my garbage."

For those who were unhappily married for a third or fourth time they again spoke of alcohol. One man's third wife was in his words "addicted to alcohol and prescription drugs" and offered the advice "you can't truly love anyone else until you love yourself. Don't marry someone to fill in the holes in your life." The pattern continued as one lady admitted ruining four marriages because of her alcoholism while another woman married an abusive alcoholic for a third time.

"You can't truly love anyone else until you love yourself. Don't marry someone to fill in the holes in your life."

The issue of trust became a factor in multiple marriages as age and cynicism led some to be unsure about the person they would marry. One man said his third wife had many unresolved issues and after ten years just moved on with another man. And another man married a woman who he said was full of promises but only wanted money and cost him over two hundred thousand dollars.

Marriage remains a mystery for many as some find happiness while others do not. But there are common threads to finding and sustaining a long term, happy marriage that include compatibility, passion, mutual respect and a willingness to give more than take.

CHAPTER 7

REGRETS

MOST OF US HAVE HEARD THE SAYING "there are two kinds of people in this world, those who learn from their own mistakes and those who learn from the mistakes of others." I assumed that people who had lived between sixty-five and one hundred years would have many regrets and that there would be much to be learned from them. But I wasn't looking for deep dark secrets and knew that not everyone would be completely forthcoming or willing to divulge their biggest mistakes and deepest regrets. This would be especially true of those who were interviewed with their spouse or another person present.

As it turned out, some people were willing to talk freely about many of their deepest regrets and mistakes. One lady said "my life is an open book so ask me anything you want." Others spoke reluctantly of regrets and were hesitant to give much detail, and some others were guarded and offered little or nothing. One lady said she made lots of mistakes and had lots of regrets but was too guarded to say much about them.

Twenty percent of those interviewed either offered no response or said they had no real regrets. The reasons for this were varied. Some simply did not want to discuss them while others said they just took life as it came. One lady gathered no regrets because of her simple philosophy of taking each day at a time. "I did what I thought I should do and left it at that. No regrets." A similar sentiment came from a lady who said "I don't think about regrets; I just lived as I went along," and a particularly happy person simply responded "I wouldn't change a thing." A response from one lady that was unintentionally comical was to repeat several times during the interview the reason she has no regrets, "I never drank, never smoked and I never swear."

"I did what I thought I should do and left it at that. No regrets."

Some people felt they were lucky in life while others said they were completely fulfilled with a very satisfied life. One lady said "I had very modest expectations so I was satisfied with what I had," and another said she had very few regrets and felt that she gained something from every experience, even the unpleasant ones.

An insightful response came from an impressive lady who said that she never encountered anything in her life that couldn't be dealt with by being "neat and sweet." Having everything in its place and being nice to others were her keys to a happy life without regret.

"Neat and sweet."

Although twenty percent had no significant regrets, eighty percent did, and of those many were substantial. In an attempt to draw people out and give them an opportunity to recount their regrets I asked three questions each with a slightly different focus. The first was "What's the biggest mistake you ever made?" I originally thought this was a relatively innocuous question, and for some it was, but for others it came across as a loaded and deeply probing question. One man in the presence of his wife glared at me and responded in an angry tone "that information will go to the grave." I didn't press him further and used that question sparingly after that experience.

The second question was more palatable for most people and garnered many and various responses, "As you look back over your life, what are your three biggest regrets?" I'm not sure why I put a number on it other than I thought some people would offer many responses and only wanted the top three. As it was, I accepted all responses. I simply asked the question and accepted every quantity of responses because I felt that if they were important enough to mention they were important enough to record. So while some people offered no regrets, for others I didn't have enough room on the page to write them all down.

The third question simply asked "If you could live your life over again what three things would you change?" I organized all the responses under regrets because all the answers were things that people either regretted doing or life circumstances they regretted having to endure.

TOP TEN REGRETS

▌ 1. Not enough education

▌ 2. Not pursuing the job I really wanted

▌ 3. Not pursuing arts more, music, dance, acting, art

▌ 4. Not "going for it." Procrastination, missed opportunities

▌ 5. Not being a better parent or family person

▌ 6. Not having enough money

▌ 7. Not travelling more

▌ 8. Getting married too young or to the wrong person

▌ 9. Not being wiser when younger

▌ 10. Not having a child or more children

By far the most common answer given when asked about regrets was "lack of education." Many people regretted not going further in school and most everyone offered unsolicited explanation about their lack of formal education, some were even apologetic. The reason for this seems to be a spillover from a time when education was less accessible or necessary to a time when it is.

A common explanation from many people was that circumstances in the earlier part of the twentieth century were difficult for many and hindered the pursuit of education. The Great Depression and WWII were difficult times that interrupted many plans for education, resources were scarce and priorities were focused on survival. Then ironically in the post war economic boom education was not as necessary for people to secure good jobs and make enough money to support a family. Jobs were available and commodities were relatively inexpensive in comparison, and as a result many people from that era did very well financially, and some felt they lived at the best time in history.

However, despite success in many areas of life, regret over a lack of education was paramount to many. It seems odd but both the bad times and subsequent good times created distraction from a focus on education that many people would come to regret. But with families to support and good jobs available, their path was set. Some would have simply liked to finish high school while others expressed a desire to get more technical training or go on to university. One lady said she would have liked to go to university but was the eighth of nine children and the resources just weren't available.

Many people from the Prairies explained that school was often far away and seen as somewhat of a luxury after basic primary school when families were struggling to run their farm or business. Most children were expected to help the family survive and every person that was raised on a farm said they were expected to work hard. Higher formal education was often seen as an unnecessary luxury for many such working class people, farmers, business owners or trades people. One lady from the Prairies who was born in the 1930s explained "the era we lived in was less conducive to education and more restricted."

"The era we lived in was less conducive to education and more restricted."

Various restrictions in the pursuit of education due to life's circumstances were a reality for many who would have liked to go to school but couldn't work it out. But for many others the lack of emphasis on the importance of education caused some to regret not making a better effort for education when they were at school. One lady regretted quitting school when she did while several people reiterated the sentiment that they wished they had worked harder when they were actually in school, not fully realizing at the time the value of the opportunity they had. Others who finished high school wished they had made a better effort to go on to university while some who started university wish they had made a greater effort to finish their degree. But it just didn't seem as important to them at the time.

The second most common answer to the question of regrets was "not pursuing the job I really wanted." Another irony of the era when jobs were either scarce or plentiful was that in many cases people felt bound to their job. One man who became a meat cutter during the 1930s said he would have liked to choose a different career but during the depression the opportunity came along and he felt lucky to even have a job. Once he became established in his trade the money, job security and responsibilities he bore bound him to it for over fifty years.

This was the case for many people who explained that they trained in one field and for reasons of practicality or necessity didn't train and work in the field they would have preferred. An auto body man explained how he didn't prefer the trade but the money was too good and he had a family to feed so didn't feel he had the freedom or opportunity to retrain. This was also the case for a man who was a plumber but would have preferred to be an electrician. Many people had unfulfilled aspirations to be a professional person, firefighter, doctor, tug boat operator, teacher, archeologist, military man, and so on. But by far the most common unfulfilled career aspiration came from those who wanted to be a nurse but didn't get the training and instead worked as care aids, support health care workers, or remained in another field entirely.

Some people fantasized about a job or work situation they think they would have liked but never had the experience. One person who worked as a lab technician said she would have preferred a more people oriented job, while another person who was a piano teacher dreamed of living and working in a lighthouse with her books and grand piano.

Unlike those who didn't have the opportunity to work in a job they preferred some people for various reasons left the job they enjoyed. Several people regretted leaving the military and others regretted leaving a business or trade they enjoyed. One lady regretted leaving a secure and satisfying job she had early in life due to her family circumstance and husband's work, and two other people expressed regret over leaving a career in broadcasting.

Another twist on regrets concerning a job came from several people who felt they retired too early and would have liked to work longer. One person missed the people and another missed the status and responsibility. For many people much of their purpose came from their career which left a void when it was gone. This was coupled by the restlessness that many felt in looking for meaningful things to do. Retirement from a job they enjoyed was a double edged sword for some.

The next most common response to regrets was not pursuing the arts more, dance, music, art, acting. Several people expressed the desire to be a professional actor, dancer or musician but due to life circumstances were never able to find a way to make it happen. One lady jokingly said "I regret not being a millionaire and that I wasn't an actor in Hollywood," but then seriously said "I should have pursued show biz more." One man wished he could have been a paid entertainer while another lady said "I picked the wrong person to marry and allowed men to prevent me from my talent. I wish I could have pursued performing arts more but my dad wouldn't allow me to and my husband discouraged me. I wasted my talent." One lady confidently said "I regret not continuing with my singing. I would have been a star." Many people were drawn by the allure of professional artistic expression and what they saw as an exotic and fulfilling life experience that they missed out on.

"I wasted my talent."

Others simply saw the arts as something that would have given their life greater fulfillment as a serious hobby. Many regretted not sticking with music lessons or pursuing whatever ability, opportunity and training they did have. Of all the arts the pursuit of music was the most common regret, playing the piano, singing, playing guitar, and so on. A surprising number of people said they would have loved to play the piano.

"I regret not continuing with my singing.
I would have been a star."

For others it wasn't just an intense appreciation for the arts but regret over their lack of ability. One lady jokingly said "I wish I had been more musical but I have three left feet and a tin ear." As the third most common response there were passionate regrets expressed and it's reasonable to conclude that regardless of ability or opportunity, the arts play a significant role in the human experience.

Looking back over their lives many people expressed regret over missed opportunity, procrastination, wishing they had accomplished more, and not "going for it" enough. Some people just said that they should have taken advantage of more opportunities while others lamented that they see in retrospect how many opportunities passed them by. This was evident as many elaborated on specific missed opportunities such as buying a house when they had the chance or investing in property that years later was very valuable and made the owners very wealthy. This was the case with many investment opportunities such as buying property at a resort which was relatively inexpensive in the 1970s, buying stock in IBM which was available to employees, or securing investments in growing companies that later made investors very wealthy. Such regret over missed opportunity was stark for those who saw others become very wealthy from taking advantage of opportunities which they themselves declined.

For others missed opportunities came in the form of experiences they can no longer pursue such as flying a plane, walking the west coast trail, going to Hong Kong, and so on. There were many. Such missed opportunities were closely tied to motivation as many people complained of problems with procrastination and not doing the things they should have. One lady reflected on her struggle saying "I wish I wasn't such a procrastinator. It has been a terrible problem for me and has kept me from a lot of experiences. I wish I would have 'gone for it' more."

"I wish I would have 'gone for it' more."

Many people talked of unfulfilled aspirations saying "I wish I had accomplished more," or as one man put it "I should have done more in lots of ways." One lady lamented "I fulfilled my aspirations but wish I had higher aspirations," and a man said "my goals weren't lofty enough. I should have set my sights higher but I had a low self concept. I was a stutterer and stammered when I was young." Similar sentiments were echoed by many others who openly regretted not setting loftier goals in their career, investments, relationships, and personal achievements.

"I should have done more in lots of ways."

Looking back on life many people openly wished they could have had a more "go for it" attitude. Some felt they were lazy and should have worked harder while others talked about being subdued and not strong enough. Some people simply expressed a desire to have had more energy and others wished they were more passionate about things. Similar sentiments were phrased slightly differently as people expressed regrets like "I was not aggressive enough in choosing my path," "I should have been more focused on what I wanted and went for it," and "I should have been more decisive." Others added "I wish I had been tougher about things," and "I wish I wasn't afraid to take risks when I was younger."

"I should have been more focused on what I wanted and went for it."

All these sentiments were summed up by one man in his eighties who said "I wasn't aggressive enough. I just let things fall into place. I wish I wasn't so passive and more assertive. I wish I had more drive and desires but instead I let life drift by me." Another man in his late eighties dying from lung disease said about his regrets "if I had a chance to do it over, I would do what I did but do it better."

"If I had a chance to do it over, I would do what I did but do it better."

Although being a better parent and family person was the fifth most common response for regrets it garnered the most comments and elaboration. Being a parent is perhaps the most regret laden and guilt producing experience one can have and this is especially true when children were mistreated and not given a healthy and happy start in life. It was noted earlier that many people carried childhood trauma with them all their lives and spoke vividly of it even in their advanced years. The impressions burned in their minds during their formative years became part of their makeup. But equally lasting is the knowledge that one's own children weren't treated properly, and many parents spoke with deep regret about such feelings.

Many people made general statements without much elaboration wishing they had been a better parent, while others were more specific saying they wished they had been more patient, more affectionate, more loving, stricter, or more lenient. But many regrets ran deeper. A frequent regret was not spending enough time with the kids, especially when they were younger, and for most this also meant quality and fun time. One lady said "I should have spent more time playing with my own kids," and another said "I regret not laughing more at my child's antics. I was embarrassed when I should have laughed." Several people explained that it seems so simple to see in retrospect but they weren't able to see it at the time. One lady simply said "I wish I had taken my kids to the beach more."

"I regret not laughing more at my child's antics. I was embarrassed when I should have laughed."

Many dads bore their share of guilt and regret as some were absentee fathers who were preoccupied, disinterested or separated from the family. They all expressed a deep sense of regret over not being the father their children needed. One dad said "I would have done more with my son and participated with him more." Several mothers expressed regret over their husband's lack of fathering skills saying "I wish my husband had spent more time with the children," and "I wish my husband had been more affectionate with the kids and wasn't so harsh at times."

"I would have done more with my son and participated with him more."

It emerged clearly in this research that there are many broken hearted mothers who deeply regret the way their children were treated. One lady was almost brought to tears as she spoke of having her young son's dog put to sleep because she didn't want to pay for the cure. The cost seemed onerous at the time but pales in comparison to her son's broken heart and the lifelong regret she bears.

Another mother regrets that she didn't pursue the help her son needed to cope with his learning disability. One mother from a small town regretted not preparing her children properly for the outside world while another wished she had diversified their lives better. The pain was palpable for one mother who shared "I wish my sick daughter hadn't tried to kill herself and

I wish I hadn't told her to go ahead. She gave up a baby for adoption then told me she hates me."

"I wish my sick daughter hadn't tried to kill herself, and I wish I hadn't told her to go ahead."

One lady regretted not being as affectionate to her daughter as she was with her boys and another reflected on being harder on one daughter over the other. The issue of favoritism came up several times as some parents were closer to one child over another, had greater expectations of one child over another, held their children to different standards, or looked after a needy child at the expense of the others. One father explained his dilemma saying "I should have been tougher on my kids and tried to help my son more. We spent too much time and money on our addict son, gave him too much at times (rent and money) when we should have helped our other son more." A similar story came from a lady who said "I wish I wasn't so hard with my oldest daughter and neglected my children. It's the biggest regret I will ever have. I wish I hadn't pandered to my sick daughter and neglected the others."

*"We spent too much time and money on our addict son...
when we should have helped our other son more."*

Drugs and alcohol played a regretful role for many parents as one man said "I wish I was a better dad but I went to the bar too much." An alcoholic husband caused one lady to lament that as a result her kids were terribly abused and deprived, and a recovering alcoholic shared "I wish I was a better mom when my son was younger but I let alcohol control my life for too long." Such regret is compounded in such cases when the parent sees the child follow the same pattern of addiction and destruction. One lady said if she could live her life over again she wouldn't drink and shared the regret of "putting my children through what they went through."

"I wish I was a better dad but I went to the bar too much."

Neglect and misplaced priorities also created many regrets for those too busy to spend quality time with their family. Many people shared how they were just too busy working when their kids were young and missed out on time spent bonding with them. An insightful lady said "I was very busy and my priorities were wrong at times. I spent too much time doing rather than being. I wish I had spent more quality time with my kids," and a dad said "I wish I was a more compassionate dad, more affectionate, and spent more time with the kids when they were young, but my job came first."

"I spent too much time doing rather than being."

For some it was a more self indulgent neglect as one lady shared that she wishes they had spent more time travelling with the family rather than as a couple and that her husband had spent more time with the kids rather than golfing. Many ladies said their husband wasn't the father they would have liked.

Some parents were so concerned with meeting their children's material needs they missed out on the relationship aspect of raising children. "I wish I had been more patient and understanding with the kids rather than being so concerned with their material needs" is what one mother shared. Another mother shared a lesson she had learned the hard way saying "I wish I had been a better parent and passed on better values to my kids. I spent too much time pursuing material things, and they are doing same thing—pursuing material things. I wish I had known then that it's better to sit on an old couch and relate to someone than to sit on a new couch by yourself."

"I wish I had known then that it's better to sit on an old couch and relate to someone than to sit on a new couch by yourself."

Other family regrets include one lady who was taken in by the promises of a young man and at age twenty-one gave up a baby for adoption. She explained her 'no win' situation and the years of heartache that followed. Another lady admitted her mistake of bringing her dad to live with her family after her mom died saying it changed her family dynamic in a negative way. And a somewhat less serious regret but an issue for several people came from a lady who said she wishes she had been a better house keeper and not kept such a messy house.

It has been mentioned in a previous chapter that many people suffered from childhood poverty, but some also listed it as regret. Explaining the mental difficulties of coming from a family that struggled and didn't have much, one lady said she wished she had more money and resources as a child. Another lady, the youngest of seven children, had a sick father and couldn't remember having any toys. This sentiment was echoed by another lady who regretted seeing her parents struggle so much during the Great Depression and said several times during the interview in a tone reminiscent of the warning to Caesar about the Ides of March "remember the hungry thirties."

"Remember the hungry thirties."

Not surprisingly money was a factor for many people who regretted not having the resources they would have liked throughout their lives. Many people simply regretted not having more money and better finances and having to endure years of working and struggling to raise their family. Life wasn't very comfortable for many people living with constant financial pressure. One stay at home mom mentioned her general lack of financial security and deeply regretted not contributing money to the household. The most stark answer came from a lady who simply looked at the floor and said of her regrets "hard times; no money."

"Hard times; no money."

Many others regretted that they didn't better manage the money they did have. Some were perhaps frivolous at times or self indulgent, but this regret was especially difficult for those who didn't properly plan for retirement. More than a few people said "I wish I had invested money and set myself up for retirement better."

"I wish I had invested money and set myself up for retirement better."

Another fairly common regret came from those who wished they had travelled more. One person wished he had travelled more when he was younger, before the wife, job and kids, to see the world through the eyes of a young person beginning life rather than a retiree looking back on life. Many other people would have simply liked to explore the planet we live on more, and one man regretted that he didn't travel more with his wife before she died, something that only really struck him in retrospect.

Failed marriages caused countless regrets for many people so it's not surprising that getting married too young or being married to the wrong person ranked in the top ten regrets. And many were willing to elaborate. One lady said she wished she had been more educated about marital issues before she got married.

Many people simply said they got married too young. One lady who said she went from her father's house to her husband's house said "I wish I would not have been such a 'yes' person to my dad and then my husband." And another lady recounted her extreme experience saying "I dropped out of school so young, was married at eighteen and gave myself over. I lost 'me' completely. I doused myself with gas and lit a match due to post partum depression."

"I dropped out of school so young, was married at eighteen and gave myself over. I lost 'me' completely."

Quite a few people said they should have chosen a spouse more carefully, been more discerning, and dated more before making their decision. Some people would have liked more time as a single person and several others said they shouldn't have ever got married at all and if they could do it again would have stayed single for life.

One lady candidly stated "I picked the wrong men," and another regretted "marrying a couple of drunks." More than a few people regretted getting married to the wrong person but regretted even more staying too long to try to save a doomed marriage. For many this involved living with abuse, infidelity, mistreatment of children and a myriad of other forms of dysfunction. Some second marriages were also disastrous as many people went from one failed relationship to another. One lady summed up her regrets by saying "I wouldn't have married the men I married because they just suited my hang-ups at the time."

"I wouldn't have married the men I married because they just suited my hang-ups at the time."

This same lady went on to say "I wish I had learned more about myself earlier," which was the next most common regret, to be wiser younger. Many people used the cliché "I wish I knew then what I know now," but others said "I wish I had a better sense of myself when I was younger." One lady said "I wish I wasn't so immature and naïve when I was younger. I felt inferior to my mom." Similar sentiments were expressed in various ways as people spoke of wishing they had more confidence and wisdom at an early age, being more emotionally balanced, having more self esteem, and not being so shy and reserved when younger. One lady laughed and said "I'm very outgoing now."

"I wish I had a better sense of myself when I was younger."

Rounding out the top ten is the regret to have had a child or more children. Not surprisingly some people regretted not having any children at all and one lady said she deeply regretted missing the opportunity. Another lady for medical reasons was only able to have one child and wanted more. What was somewhat surprising, however, were the people who had many children but wanted even more. One lady had three but wanted six, another lady had five and wanted more and yet another lady had seven children but six were boys and she wanted more girls.

Regrets were many and varied as people verbalized their 'woulda-shoulda-couldas,' and after the top ten there were still some fairly frequent responses, some serious and some just musings about things that could have been better.

A few people expressed regret over bad business deals that in some cases caused serious financial setback. Many times it was an investment that was supposed to generate money and in the end cost a great deal of money. One person spoke of a business deal with a brother-in-law that started out as the next biggest thing and ended up quite the opposite. One lady said "I wish we hadn't bought a bowling alley with all our savings and equity. We lost it all." Another expressed regret over the stress of owning and operating an orchard for twenty years while others experienced bad real estate decisions such as selling a house then regretting it later but unable to get something similar because of a rise in prices. One man regretted his decision saying "I sold my condo too cheap three years ago, now I rent."

When asked about her regrets, one lady offered only one word, "alcohol." Not surprisingly, quite a few people expressed regret over alcohol. For some it was regret over partying too much in their youth and the resulting missed opportunity while for others it was too much alcohol in the family, at work, or as a lifestyle. Alcohol began as fun for lots of people then became a problem for some. One man said "I partied too much and should have done more in lots of ways," and another said "I squandered too much time and money and drank too much." Another man voiced his regret saying "I should have spent less on foolishness and partying and smartened up earlier in life."

"Alcohol."

Many people let drinking become a problem for much of their life. One lady who destroyed her relationships and regretted the example she set for her kids said "I wish I had gotten sober earlier. I was fifty and regret the things I did when under the influence." This was echoed by a lady who wished she hadn't drank saying "I regret allowing people to do harmful things to me, putting myself in dangerous situations, and putting my children through what they went through."

A sober and impressive man in his seventies said "I regret drinking too much and not quitting earlier. I could have done more had I been different and not drank. I regret my relationship with my sons because of my booze. One son hasn't talked to me in ten years." This sentiment was echoed by more than a few people as one man said "my biggest regret was my addictions. I wish I was a better dad. I was a terrible dad."

"I regret my relationship with my sons because of my booze. One son hasn't talked to me in ten years."

Some people regretted having so many obligations and not being able to pursue their own interests like one lady who said "I wish I could have changed my circumstances to what I wanted," or another who said "I allowed other people to run my life and should have taken control of my own life, goals and future." One lady complained that she let men prevent her from her talent and another said she regretted letting go of things she was good at when she was younger. Such complaints didn't come across like selfishness but were the regrets of people who consistently put themselves last then looked back with regret on their restricted circumstances and unfulfilled aspirations.

A hard working farm mom said "I wanted more free time. I worked too much, all work and no play." This was a fairly common complaint as many people spent their lives fulfilling what was expected of them. Most just accepted their lot at the time, and some even played into it. One lady said "I wish I wasn't such a people pleaser" while another said "I wish I had more independence to pursue my hobbies. I was third, husband, kids, me." She added "I wish I had more opportunity to do things for myself rather than just doing what was expected of me." The strongest emotion came from a lady who said "I regret spending too much effort on work and family and not enough on 'me'. I should have been a writer. I would have loved to play music and take more piano lessons. I took them then quit. I had a stress related nervous breakdown from all the pressure."

"I worked too much, all work and no play."

Health issues were a major regret for some people as age revealed the years of failing to maintain a healthy body. Many people simply said they wish they had exercised more and lived a healthier lifestyle. More than a few people regretted the implications of smoking for many years, and some were permanently attached to an oxygen tank. Several people spoke of hurting their body through years of hard physical work, and one widow said she wished her husband had looked after himself better because their life together was cut short.

Somewhat related to health and exercise issues were those who wished they had pursued sports and athletics more seriously, even professionally. One man said he wished he could have been a professional golfer, another said basketball and another cricket. For most it was a musing of 'what if' rather than something that was a real possibility, but it was also an acknowledgment that we need to take advantage of opportunities when they present themselves, in this case when we're young and healthy, otherwise they pass by. One lady regretted not pursuing her skating to see how far she could have gone. She had a satisfying career as a skating coach but always wondered how much success she herself might have had. A similar story came from a professional boxer who declined an opportunity to train in New York and always wondered what he might have done.

Marital issues came up consistently as the source of many regrets and more than a few people said they wish they had been a better spouse. One lady regretted that she had been interested in another man while another acknowledged her mistake in "thinking the grass is greener." A somewhat enlightened response came from a lady who said "I wish I had been smarter about handling my husband to have a less stormy marriage. He was unhappy so I went to counseling." The death of a spouse seemed to illuminate and intensify regrets and include a widow who said "I wish I had been kinder to my husband," or another who said without elaborating "I should have kissed my husband more."

"I should have kissed my husband more."

Many men willingly admitted their shortcomings as a spouse, which for many meant taking their wife for granted. A widower reflected that he wishes he had been the husband his wife deserved, especially earlier in their marriage. Another regretted discouraging his wife from pursuing her dream of being a flight attendant leaving her with a lifelong unfulfilled aspiration. His regret intensified after her death. Yet another man who worked very hard for a family he ignored and eventually lost candidly admitted "I took things for granted, my wife and kids. I wish I was more understanding and tolerant, and less self-righteous and hard."

"I took things for granted, my wife and kids. I wish I was more understanding and tolerant, and less self-righteous and hard."

Many people regretted that they worked too much and often didn't realize until later the damage it did to their family and personal lives. A typical response was "I wish I was closer to my kids but I worked too much," and "I was an absentee parent because of my job." Some resolve and understanding came later in life for most who said things like "I wish I wasn't a workaholic," "I wish I had more balance between work and fun time," and the typical farm response, "we worked all the time and never had time for much else." One lady who looked after her home and family then lost her husband to an early death said "I wish my husband hadn't worked so much; he worked too hard."

"I was an absentee parent because of my job."

A surprising number of people regretted not seeing or knowing one or both of their parents. One man lamented being raised in an orphanage not having or knowing any parents. For many others it was having one or more parent die at an early age, several before they were old enough to have known them, and some after the age of four or five. One lady said "I wish I could have known my dad or had a dad. I was teased about it." Another lady deeply regretted going to boarding school and not living with her family or feeling like she really knew them when she returned.

"I wish I could have known my dad or had a dad.
I was teased about it."

Related to this were those who wish they had shown more concern for loved ones before their death. One lady said that at nineteen she had an argument with her dad and didn't speak to him for six years but later regretted not spending enough time with her parents before they died. Another lady regretted being unkind to her dad one time when he was ill before he died, and another simply wanted to hug her mom but then said "she wasn't like that." One man's regret was "I didn't show enough respect at times to my parents and I didn't help my parents enough," and another man just regretted that he didn't get more information about the family and family members before they died.

For many people the finality of the death of a loved one brought with it emotions around wishing they had handled their relationships better. This was especially the case for a lady who said "I wish I had spent more time closer to people before they died," then cried during the interview as she shared her deepest regret. "A neighborhood boy committed suicide. He had wanted to talk to me but I didn't take the time."

"A neighborhood boy committed suicide.
He had wanted to talk to me but I didn't take the time."

Looking back over their lives, many people expressed regret as they realized the consequences of worry, self doubt, and fear. Some just complained of being a worrier while others struggled with being "too cautious" or having a "low self concept." One person wished for more self confidence while another wished he had been willing to take risks at times. This severely hindered one man who said of not advancing at his job "I resisted promotion and I don't know why" or another who said of changing jobs "I regret thinking I couldn't do it."

"I regret thinking I couldn't do it."

Fear was a menace in many lives as one lady simply said "I wish I didn't live in fear." Another elaborated saying "I wish I had dealt with fear earlier in my life. I feared success as much as failure," and a sad admission from another lady who said "I still carry the fear of failure at age seventy-seven."

"I wish I had dealt with fear earlier in my life."

Given the era in which most people lived, WWII factored into most people's experiences resulting in many women coming to North America as war brides. For some this was a positive experience, but not so for many others who found themselves in a strange country away from their loved ones and familiar surroundings. One lady bluntly said "I'm sorry I didn't marry an Englishman and stay in England." Another spoke of her excitement in coming to North America after WWII, the supposed land of opportunity, and ended up with her new husband in a shack on the Prairies struggling to survive the brutal winters.

Others who came to North America immediately following WWII (and others in the following years) said they regretted it at first but grew to like their new home. However, this was certainly not the case for one lady who when asked about her regrets said without hesitation "I cried on the plane all the way. If I could live my life over again I would never have left England."

Many regrets involved family or personal issues as some people regretted things like not becoming a Christian earlier, or not getting a driver's license earlier, or at all. Many women from this era didn't drive at all, didn't drive very much, or didn't get a driver's license until later in life. This was yet another form of subjugation they accepted at the time but regretted looking back.

More family related regrets came up beginning with marital breakup, a life altering event for those who went through it. Given some of the difficult family circumstances recounted above, many marriages were destined to breakup, but some others wish their marriage had survived. One man candidly admitted that he caused his marital breakup by infidelity and wished he hadn't. And a lady regretted walking out on her husband after a heated argument.

Others regretted not getting married at all, never finding the right person to share and fulfill their life. For one man his fiancé was killed and he regretted not being able to find another compatible mate. He said he's still looking at age sixty-nine. Another lady who never married said "I wish I had kids, maybe, or a husband. I wish I hadn't gone to an all-girls school and had a domineering mother because I didn't meet or relate to men."

There were those who complained of having too many siblings, yet for others their regret was not having any. Several people expressed the regret of never knowing the feeling of having a brother or sister to be raised with and relate to throughout their lives.

The remaining regrets didn't really fit any category. Some were funny, some seemingly less important, but all were important to those who shared so they are presented here individually in no particular order.

More than one person regretted not learning another language, while another regretted not being more involved in social and political issues. For another it was falling away from faith while for others it was waiting too long to return to their faith.

Several people expressed regret over never owning a home. Some had a chance and didn't take advantage of it while others were never able to work it out.

Personal issues continued to come up as one person jokingly regretted "being born" while another regretted "being born too soon" and would have liked to enjoy the world the way it is now rather than in her day. Along the same line another man regretted that he isn't going to live another one hundred years.

One person half jokingly said "I wish I had more brains," but for others regrets were more serious like one man who bluntly regretted being so stubborn and thick headed. Another said he wishes he had accepted people more. One lady wished she had been nicer to people and not said so many nasty things. For another it was gossip as one man deeply regretted saying too much about another person and paying a big price for it.

"I wish I had more brains."

Past issues continued to come up as one lady said she took her childhood memories, shut the door and nailed it. Another lady listed off a bad childhood, lack of appetite and being too thin, marital breakup due to her husband's affair and the resulting depression. Then she said "I can't cry. Maybe I have shut it off."

"I can't cry. Maybe I have shut it off."

Childhood issues were never very far from anyone as one man said he wished his dad had been stricter and not let him do whatever he wanted, and a lady still suffers the affects of being mistreated by others at school, enough to list it as regret. One lady said "I wish I had more encouraging people in my life and I wish my mom was more affectionate," and another regretted "too many people telling me they did better at my age."

Several people had very few regrets and explained how they reached resignation about their difficulties. One lady reasoned "I haven't heard from my oldest daughter since she was sixteen (in the 1960's). I don't know what happened to her and assume she's dead. She was into drugs. But I have no regrets. Everything is a learning experience." Another lady said she believes in karma and simply attributed any hardship to something she might have done in a past life.

"I wish I had been luckier."

Some people had age related regrets. For one it was moving in to the care home and for another it was feeling like "I'm a burden to my family now and I don't like it." One man simply said he wished he had enjoyed his life more while another summed up her life and regrets by saying "I wish I had been luckier."

By definition luck is something we can't control and some people certainly weren't very fortunate in the way things worked out. But the subject of the next chapter is advice to young people intended to help them avoid some of the regrets recounted here.

CHAPTER 8

ADVICE TO YOUNG PEOPLE

IF YOU'RE A YOUNG PERSON reading this book to gain some insights from the life experience of older people this is the money chapter because it speaks directly to you. Responses are presented primarily in their own words and are direct but with little finger wagging. They have all had their trials and made mistakes.

In many ways this chapter is a mirror image of the previous chapter on regrets because people answer the questions based on the things they have learned from their own mistakes and observations. And as with previous chapters the answers are somewhat arbitrarily categorized but done so in an attempt to bring some organization to many and varied responses.

TOP TEN PIECES OF ADVICE

- 1. Get an education
- 2. Think things through, have a plan, set goals
- 3. Get some kind of career, vocation, trade or training
- 4. Find the right mate
- 5. Have good morals, honest, respectful, good character
- 6. Find out what you enjoy and pursue it
- 7. Avoid debt and live within your means
- 8. Have a positive attitude and do the best you can in everything you do
- 9. Know yourself, establish yourself, and be your own person
- 10. Work Hard

Because lack of formal education was the most common regret expressed it is not surprising that the most common piece of advice to young people is to get an education. For many people it was the first word out of their mouth when asked to offer advice, yet few felt the need to elaborate. Many acknowledged that education is much more important in today's world than it was in theirs. One person gave a warning saying "get a good education or you will set yourself up to struggle, sometimes for life. It affects everything." Other comments were similar in nature urging young people to have a "desire for education" and to "do something with it." One person simply said "get as much education as you can. I can't impress this too much."

"Get as much education as you can. I can't impress this too much."

Many people stressed the importance of thinking things through and formulating a life plan with definite goals. It was emphasized many times in similar ways. The first issue was for young people to resist their impulses to be rash and to really "think things over before you decide." Based on their trials older people urged younger people to "stop and think before jumping in," "really think things over before doing it. Think first then act," and "go easy and think it over. Don't make rash decisions."

The thrust of their advice was to look at options and make good choices, something especially difficult for impulsive young people. One person was blunt in saying "you have choices, so make them," while another said "decide what you want to do and do it when you're younger rather than older."

"You have choices, so make them."

In making choices and setting goals one person offered the caution "don't worry about climbing the ladder. Pursue goals that are worthwhile." Several people spoke of balancing the head and heart. One person said "follow your heart but let your head have a say," while another said "balance your heart and your head fifty-fifty."

"Follow your heart but let your head have a say."

Once the choices are made there was plenty of advice about forming a plan and sticking to it. "Set goals and work towards them knowing it will take time" was what one person said, and another added "don't expect things immediately. Plan and be prepared to wait and work for what you get." Some others urged that a plan also needs a time table in order to be successful.

"Set goals and work towards them knowing it will take time."

Several analogies about setting a life plan were offered as one pragmatic man said "life is like going into business, plan it out," and another said "some people have destination sickness; they are here but don't know where they're going." A flight analogy was used several times with one person saying "if the pilot doesn't know where he's going then he should land the plane until he has a flight plan."

"Some people have destination sickness; they are here but don't know where they're going."

The strongest statement came from a man who mixed several analogies saying "life is what you make of it. We are master of our own destiny so don't drift. Don't be a victim of circumstance but steer your own ship. Set goals, formulate a plan, and live within your means. Life is like a staircase. You can't step from the bottom to the top but need to take steps. If necessary, change your flight plan. Life is much like that. Do what works." I felt like saying amen at the end of what he said.

The third most popular piece of advice for young people was to get some kind of trade, vocation or training. This is perhaps obvious but the general thrust was that getting some kind of skill and a good job as early as possible is a key element in building a fulfilling life. As one man put it "get a trade; get set up so you can build a good life," and another said "get a vocation early. Set yourself up early." One man suggested young people get some kind of vocational guidance and testing to assist in choosing the right vocation, and another said to young people "get training and education; focus on your bent."

More than a few people promoted the armed forces saying things like "consider the service for pay, travel, education," and some promoted their favorite branches saying "join the army, for learning, discipline, organization, and defense of the country," or "join the navy for the discipline and opportunity." For many people the service was much more than just a job. It was a life changing experience as one man said "I went in a boy and came out a man."

The general idea in advising young people to get established in a vocation was to encourage them to think more long term because older people understand how much more it means looking back than it does looking forward. When you're young and carefree long term planning doesn't seem to matter as much, but looking back it is most important. Getting a vocation and good job early in life was a triumph for those who managed it and regret for those who didn't. Either way the advice was the same to "get a piece of paper, some kind of trade or training," and "get a trade that is steady, stable and has a pension." Another person wisely said "get out there and study your craft. You'll get as much as you put in."

This sage advice coincided with those who encouraged lifelong learning of all kinds. Some people simply said "learn everything you can," "learn from your experiences" and "never stop learning." As one man put it, "diverse knowledge is key," and another said "take classes on anything you can." One man brought it all together by encouraging young people to "have resources to fall back on and training. Develop as a person so you'll always be looked after."

"Never stop learning."

This put a much broader and more practical focus on education with the idea that "learning is an ongoing process so learn wherever and whenever you can." That's what true education is. Others advise young people to "learn to do lots of things. It's nice to know a lot, so learn all the time. Learn everything you can," and "absorb information of every kind and keep on through your life."

"Absorb information of every kind and keep on through your life."

A slightly different focus came from one person who said "always try to learn as much as you can, but especially about people." This affects every aspect of our lives. One person pointed out that as we learn about people we can also "learn from the examples of others." This is done by both observation and interaction. One man said "learn from people and people learn from you. Exchange information," the broader implication being that exchange of information is the type of education that is available everywhere to all who take advantage of it. One man put it succinctly saying "learn something at every job. Be a good learner. Always be moving forward in life. Learn something new every day."

> *"Always try to learn as much as you can,*
> *but especially about people."*

Many people had advice to give on marriage and relationships as a key component in building a meaningful life and avoiding problems. The most common caution said many times in similar ways was "choose a mate carefully and wait until you're sure about the right person." Compatibility was a primary reason given for long and happy marriages so it's not surprising that many people said to find a compatible mate, someone on the same page about most of life's issues. "Find a compatible mate and person. Family background has a lot to do with it," "find someone who supports and loves you," and "find a partner who has similar interests, character, continuity, and consistency."

There is no doubt that generally speaking the women of the generation interviewed suffered much more from bad marriages than men and as a result had very strongly worded advice for young women, specifically to shop around and look for a suitable mate. "Don't take second best in a partner. Be discerning and make sure you're sure." Quite a few ladies gave their advice as a warning saying things like "be careful about a partner. Decide what you want and know what you expect from a relationship," "choose your partner carefully, same faith, same ethics, good work ethic, communication, cooperation," and "be careful. Find a partner with a stable background who has a vision."

More warnings were given to young women including "don't be more in love with getting married than being married; be truthful with yourself and your partner and don't marry the first person that comes along," and "be careful about relationships and make sure it's for you. It's not 'getting' married that's challenging, but 'being' married." A poignant statement came from a woman who had suffered difficulties and said "don't get married because you don't want to be alone because you can be alone and married and that's worse." The pain of abusive marriages also came through as one woman cautioned "make sure your husband is honest with you. Don't be a door mat like I was. It's easy to fall in love but harder to stay in love so don't be taken in by infatuation."

"Don't get married because you don't want to be alone because you can be alone and married and that's worse."

One lady said "make sure you marry the love of your life," as though she might have married her second choice, and another said somewhat surprisingly "make sure you love the man you marry." It's difficult to think that two people would marry without being in love but it was a sentiment expressed by more than a few people and prompted one lady to say "marry for the right reason."

Don't be a door mat like I was.

Insights continued from ladies who said things like "pick a nice person as a mate," "make sure you like the person you marry," "find someone who cherishes you," and "pick a man who is good to his mom." Several people encouraged young people to live common law before marriage to get to know their prospective mate better before marriage, but others cautioned the opposite saying "don't live with someone before you're married," and "marriage is the beginning of a life together, not just living together."

"Make sure you love the man you marry."

A common thread for many women was they felt that they married too young and wanted to caution young women against it. The sentiment was expressed by many women in many ways like "find a good mate and wait until he comes along and don't be in a hurry to get married." Speaking from their own negative experience several ladies said "have your freedom, don't get married too early," and "don't rush into marriage; be clear up front what you want from marriage."

Along with getting married too young many women also felt they had missed out on enjoying their young life. As a result much of the advice they gave had also to do with being free longer as one woman said "wait a bit longer to get married and do what you want when you're young because life gets serious." Others said things like "take time to think about life before marriage and kids," "get an education, travel and have fun before you get married," and "get silly things out of your life."

"Take time to think about life before marriage and kids."

"Be a good and ethical person" was the fifth most popular piece of advice as older people encouraged young people to pursue discipline, honesty, truthfulness, forgiveness, respect, manners, character, responsibility, and a sense of fairness. Such attributes form the basis of a meaningful and satisfying life. One person urged young people to "get a good foundation, morals, loyalty, and work ethic," a sentiment reiterated by many others who said things like "be straight forward and honest in everything you do," "be dependable, a person of your word," and "be good to your fellow man."

"Be straight forward and honest in everything you do."

Others elaborated on this sentiment saying things like "live a good clean life," "let your conscience be your guide," and "be a nice and likeable person." These sound familiar and perhaps even somewhat preachy, but they were given as humble and practical advice about what they see as some of the most important aspects of creating and living a healthy and happy life. One lady simply said "the golden rule leads to a happy life," and another said "if someone likes you, try to return it." A similar thought came from a person who said "treat others as friends not enemies." There were many more such pieces of advice like "be honest and kind in all you do," "be trustworthy and find trustworthy people to be around," "don't be greedy," and "have personal integrity."

"Be a nice and likeable person."

More specific responses include treating others with care and respect. One person said "be more polite and modest in your behavior," and another added "don't be so self centered and know it all, be polite, and say please and thank you. There used to be too much discipline but now there's not enough, so be self-disciplined." "Take everyone as you find them and treat them with respect. Love and respect everyone you come in contact with. Manners and respect are lacking in some young people." This came with the admonition to "see people for who they are on the inside," and "show respect for yourself and others. If everyone knew this we wouldn't even have wars." The simplest word of advice was "choose to love in all things."

"There used to be too much discipline but now there's not enough, so be self-disciplined."

A more comprehensive piece of advice came from a wise man who said "have good intentions in all you do. Treat people nicely through adversity. Ask yourself 'how important is this, really?' Don't worry too much. Write down everything you're worried about; most won't come about. Build credibility over your life. Be honest with yourself. Be honest in business."

An old fashioned sounding warning came from a person who encouraged young people to "resist temptations of the modern world," and as might be expected many people said "respect your elders." Perhaps the funniest piece of advice, although not intended to be, was "don't be a lawyer. We have too many."

Among the advice given to young people there was great emphasis on finding something you enjoy doing. One person asked "What are your main motivations? What do you enjoy?" and followed up by saying "find something that comes naturally." A similar sentiment was expressed by a person who asked "Have you given careful consideration to your gifts and abilities?" then encouraged young people saying "don't just go for pay. Find something you enjoy. Follow your passions as far as you can." Yet another person asked "Where's your heart? What do you feel drawn to?" and followed up saying "be honest with yourself." One person simply said "find what interests you and go for it," and another included a warning "decide what you would like to do and do it or you'll regret it all your life." This advice coincided with what another person said, "make up your mind what you're passionate about and be dedicated to it one hundred percent, no dithering."

"Decide what you would like to do and do it or you'll regret it all your life."

Because work represents such a huge part of most people's lives and is foundational in building a meaningful life, such advice was primarily about finding an enjoyable job or career. Examples include "pick something that appeals to you," "get a secure job that you enjoy," and "find something you enjoy that will also pay money. It helps tremendously if you really enjoy it." As a second best option one person suggested "be the best you can be and make your job fun in some way," and another said "learn to love your job and it will love you, otherwise get something else." This was reiterated by a person who said "look for a job you have a passion for. As Joseph Campbell said 'find your bliss,'" and "try as many things as you can. Be discerning and then be committed." Another man said "get a job you like or your life will be discontent. A good job that you enjoy can make your life happier."

"Get a job you like or your life will be discontent. A good job that you enjoy can make your life happier."

Many older people who had lived through both difficult times as well as prosperous times were adamant in their advice to avoid debt and live within your means. It was sage advice but sounded like many grandparents who said things like "live modestly," "live within your means, avoid credit cards and debt," and "don't buy a big item until you have the money." This was the way of the responsible older person, but it is much more difficult for most young people to live at the current standard of living without carrying debt in the form of mortgages, car payments, credit card payments and many other kinds of debt and obligation.

With that in mind the advice remained constant as older people said to younger people "the simple life is best and most rewarding," and "learn to be content with what you have." "People want more and more. Live within your means. Don't try to keep up with the Joneses."

"The simple life is best and most rewarding."

The overriding point for many older people was that the standard of living we strive to achieve and maintain is generated by our desire to create and possess more and more things. That's why one person said "don't be greedy for toys," and another said "accept what you and your husband can earn and live within that. Don't expect more and be happy with what you have." The common refrain was for young people to learn to be happy with less as the previous generation had. A credible point was made by a British lady who said "we saw lots of stuff broken during the war, so it wasn't worth going into debt to buy things that were so vulnerable to being destroyed."

Other people offered small but valuable pieces of advice saying "learn to dislike debt, pay bills before pleasure," "look after your credit rating (very important)," "spend less than you make," and "learn the value of money."

Another piece of advice most of us have heard from grandparents is to always do your best and have a positive attitude. Many older people have said that it doesn't matter what you do but "aim to be the best in what you do," and "do things well; put out effort." Regardless of one's circumstances or abilities, many older people insisted "do the best you can with what you have," "do the best job you can do at everything, and do it a bit extra. Show that you care in all you do."

"Show that you care in all you do."

This advice coincides with the idea that "a lot of things depend on your attitude." One person boldly stated that "a positive attitude means everything," and others made comments like "develop a positive attitude about all things," "make the best of everything," and "find a way to be happy with your achievements."

"A positive attitude means everything."

The positive mindset shouldn't be understated here because many people that had suffered through tremendous adversity were only able to come to terms with their difficulties by adopting a positive attitude and trying to make the best of difficult circumstances. Some people had great success in their lives and many others suffered adversity, but when asked how they were able to find happiness and contentment in this world virtually all of them attributed it to a positive attitude and a decision to be happy.

"Life is what you make it so have a positive mindset."

Regardless of one's start in life or difficulties that arise, many people insisted that "life is what you make it so have a positive mindset." Beyond the general statement to be positive there were some specifics such as "say to yourself 'I'm so happy, I love my life,'" "when you get up before you look in the mirror, smile and you'll have a better day," "keep a smile on your face, and help other people along the way. If you see a person without a smile, give him one of yours." By the amount of people that talked about maintaining a positive attitude and offered so many examples, it was obvious that they had spent a great deal of time thinking about how they choose to see the world and their place in it.

"If you see a person without a smile, give him one of yours."

Acceptance was also a common theme as several people made comments like "accept that things are difficult," "accept in advance what will happen and you'll do better dealing with it," and "accept things you can't change and just go with the flow." Along the same lines others said "take what you have and do the best you can with it," "learn to be happy without too much money," "live with no regrets, and do the best you can as you go along."

"Accept that things are difficult."

Living without regrets was a key piece of advice for some people in adopting and maintaining a positive mindset. This was stated very well by a person who said "live without regrets and don't be too hard on yourself or expect others to be perfect or you will be permanently frustrated. Smile a lot and be happy." Others added "forgive and forget, never hold a grudge," and "don't feel sorry for yourself."

"Don't be too hard on yourself or expect others to be perfect or you will be permanently frustrated."

A few more pieces of advice worth recounting come from people who just wanted to give young people a verbal shot in the arm by saying things like "always look on the bright side," "be optimistic in all you do," "be happy in whatever you're doing," and "don't worry too much." This relates to the last and perhaps best piece of advice "keep smiling. Don't let things get you down. This too will pass. Always be nice."

Closely related to developing and maintaining a positive mindset many people strongly encouraged young people to establish a good sense of self as soon as possible. One person succinctly said "look at yourself and start there." Others added "know yourself first before anything and develop self confidence," "know yourself the best you can as early as you can," and "develop a good sense of yourself and your place in the world."

"Know yourself the best you can as early as you can."

Such advice stems from the feelings that many people had from having to face the world as a young person without a well established sense of self. The litany of advice given on this includes "establish yourself, figure out what you want to do and what you want to be," "know yourself and don't live in a fantasy world. Express your feelings," and "don't be too anxious to grow up. Know what you want and what you're doing."

Older people encouraged younger people to "slow down and get to know yourself first, get yourself situated, and learn how to say no." "Decide, What do I want out of life? Who do I want to be?" and "discover your needs and find how to meet them." The upshot of this advice is to "develop as an individual first, have a good sense of self, and hang on to your dreams." Another person offered lengthy encouragement saying "recognize patterns in your life and explore what you want to do. Nothing is impossible so don't limit yourself. Uncover who you are and decide who you want to be, and work on yourself."

As with previous advice, there was much given specifically from older women to younger women many of whom were not able to establish their own person before being constrained by the obligations of a husband and family. Such feelings prompted one lady to say "know yourself well so you can attract someone with the same values. Listen to your own instincts," and another lady added "be your own person but not in a selfish way, and don't lose yourself in a marriage."

"Don't lose yourself in a marriage."

Another lady urged young women to "find your own self-worth. Learn to like yourself and be your own best friend. Don't be a martyr or victim." One woman who had suffered abuse at the hands of several men said "be yourself and know that you're worth something. Don't let people put you down. Know who and what you are and be strong in that." A similar sentiment prompted one lady to quote Shakespeare saying "this above all, 'to thine own self be true.' Never lose sight of you but adjust to things as they happen. You are stronger than you think to face adversity," and another added, "be a person in your own right. Don't kowtow."

"Learn to like yourself and be your own best friend."

There were further admonitions to "be a strong and self directed individual," "be your own person, don't follow the crowd," "don't try to be what you're not," and "stand up for yourself and take pride in yourself." The encouragement continued as older people said to young people "be your own counselor, and guide yourself," and "don't be afraid to be yourself; you are your own person, unique." "Know yourself and your propensities," "meditate, and watch your thoughts go by. Love yourself as much as you can. Focus on good things and do some soul searching," and "always look for a way to improve yourself." "Be resourceful. Learn how to survive," "know and honor yourself," "listen to your warning bells and listen to your heart. Find your path to happiness and live your own life," and "find your inner strength and nurture it." Perhaps the strongest statement came from a person who said "be good and strong. Be in control of your mind at all times and in control of your happiness, then you'll be a success. If you're happy with yourself then success is achieved."

"If you're happy with yourself, then success is achieved."

Virtually everyone from this generation respects hard work. Most of them worked very hard to survive and most eventually thrived, and they expect the subsequent generations to work hard as well. Their basic message is that hard work not only teaches the value of money but more importantly it builds a certain character that can't be achieved in any other way. Such thinking comes through loud and clear in comments like "learn how to work hard and enjoy it," and "work for everything you get. Earn everything, and respect material things." Others added "don't be afraid to get your hands dirty," "pay your dues with discipline, honesty, and hard work," and "put maximum effort and enthusiasm into whatever job you have and work hard."

"Pay your dues with discipline, honesty, and hard work."

Much advice was offered about finding a job and working hard at it. Stringing the comments together from numerous people reads like a plan that young people might follow. "Go where the work is and make the best of it," "get a job and work hard, don't expect something for nothing," "build up, start at the bottom and work hard," "be self-disciplined, work hard for your employer," "do a fair day's work for a fair day's pay," "don't expect things immediately, plan and be prepared to wait and work for what you get," and "don't expect so much without working for it. You won't have what your parents have right away. It takes time." The preceding is the life plan that some of the people interviewed followed and one that they want to pass on to the subsequent generations.

Yet the irony for those people who worked so hard is that many of them felt they had sacrificed their dreams and missed the opportunity to follow their heart. So while they encourage young people to work hard many people also advise young people to go for it and follow their dreams. One person summed it up saying "follow your passions and take advantage of your 'loves' while you have the chance." "Go for it, spread your wings, and follow your dreams," was what one person urged young people to do while others said things like "try to live your life to the fullest," "always follow your heart, and if you have a goal go for it," and "go for whatever you can."

"Go for it, spread your wings, and follow your dreams."

Such advice was based largely on their own unfulfilled aspirations and what many would change if they could do it over again. They said "be pro-active about things," "follow your instinct, listen to your gut feeling, don't get to fifty and wish you had done things," and "don't waste your time."

Most young people feel like they have lots of time but the perspective looking back is that youth passes quickly prompting many to say things like "don't be too reserved as a youngster, just go for it," "make the most of your young lives," and "write out your dreams and do something about it." The advice continued sounding like a pep talk as people said "be open to life, embrace it, look for your blessing, something that enhances you," "be adventurous," and "be willing to try things." And as for possibilities one person urged "nothing is impossible so don't limit yourself."

"Nothing is impossible so don't limit yourself."

Older people agreed that opportunities are most plentiful for young people and that youthful exuberance needs to be exercised to the fullest. A common refrain was "don't be afraid to move to where the opportunity is," and "seize opportunities when you have them because they could go. Don't put things off. Do them now." This coincided with admonitions like "run your own life," "admit your mistakes," "don't close any doors," and "learn to recognize opportunity and believe you can do it."

Many older people spoke of fear and hesitation that held them back and said if they could do it again they would not worry so much about what other people think or about taking risks. This brought a flurry of advice about overcoming inner obstacles. One person boldly said "don't work from fear. Recognize your abilities beyond what you think." But given the previous advice by many to strive for some kind of security the irony couldn't be missed when another said "don't be overly concerned about security, like I was. Don't worry about failure."

"Don't work from fear."

Perhaps looking back it's easier to encourage young people not to worry so much, but whether they could have done it themselves given the uncertainty they faced remains in question. Nevertheless they continued to urge young people as though now cheering from the sidelines saying "if you want your dreams to come true you have to take risks, determine what your dreams are then be prepared to do what is required to fulfill them," "don't be afraid of making mistakes because you will learn from them and be better for it," and "don't underestimate your abilities. Don't be afraid to try. Make it happen. Don't be afraid to take a chance or change. Listen to your instincts."

Similar advice was plentiful as people continued saying "don't be afraid to fail but be confident," "don't be intimidated but forge ahead," "don't worry about what people think" and "pick what you want to do and do it despite criticism." Everyone can relate to what it feels like to resist doing something out of fear of failure or criticism and many older people had suffered life altering consequences as a result. This prompted one person to say "you are capable of more than you think so don't be a victim of your own fear."

The overriding point that older people wanted to pass on is that they wish they had known earlier in life that inner strength overcomes many of the so-called hurdles that they felt prevented them from doing things.

"You are capable of more than you think so don't be a victim of your own fear."

Many older people said that inner strength is found and fostered through spirituality prompting responses like "search for an understanding of spirituality, be a good and ethical person," "recognize the importance of having a spiritual life and practicing your faith, look to God for guidance," and "faith is important to a meaningful life. Respect your creator. Appreciate the grandeur of the universe. Develop a good sense of yourself and your place in the world."

The message to young people is to "develop your relationship with God," and "get right with God and get spiritual things right first." What follows from this is God's leading as people said "get on your knees and talk to God," and "ask God to lead and expect him to do it."

"Get on your knees and talk to God."

For some people their advice about spirituality was fairly general while for others it was a particular faith. Due primarily to the demographics of those interviewed Christianity was most common by far. One person said "find Jesus Christ first, before all, make God your priority and head of your household," and several others encouraged young people to "get some wisdom from the bible," and "read the bible and live by it."

Many people who spoke of a spiritual grounding also encouraged fellowship with a community of other likeminded people saying things like "seek a religion early and try to live by it," "find a good church and get a spiritual grounding," and "go to church and establish proper values and meaning."

Some people had little or no use for spiritual values, but for others it was one of the most important aspects of life. They encouraged young people to "be patient and trust in God, you are not alone," and "have a love, respect and reverence for God. It's necessary for a full and meaningful life." This is born of their belief that "faith is the glue that holds your life together," so "have a belief and faith that will sustain you despite the natural circumstances and difficulties in life."

"Have a belief and faith that will sustain you despite the natural circumstances and difficulties in life."

Financial issues ranked very high in advice as many older people implored young people to "be careful with finances, budget properly and be smart," "don't waste money, get yourself set up financially," and "find a way to work it out."

Savings was important to most people as well saying things like "pay yourself first," and "start a savings account early and save your money. It's very important." Others added "live modestly," and "have a rainy day fund to protect yourself." Protection through savings was especially important as retirement arrived prompting many people to say "protect your old age funds as soon as you can," "plan ahead for security," "set yourself up financially for later in life," and "save some money for retirement."

For most people this was done by investments, particulary land, and some advised young people to "learn about investments and finances," then "save money and invest." Business investments were very successful for some people but not so much for others causing one person to say "in business, watch the overhead. Don't rely on luck but good management."

The majority of people in this study invested in real estate and did very well at it prompting the advice to "save to buy a home," "buy a house no matter how hard it is," and "don't waste money on cars but invest your money." For most people financial independence was very important to their peace of mind, and this was especially true later in life as their earning power declined and was eventually gone. The insight they passed on from this is "don't be dependent on anyone else for finances," and "every person should work to be financially independent."

"Every person should work to be financially independent."

Given all the people who talked of working together with a spouse to build a life, it's ironic that personal independence was also a common theme in giving advice to young people. Many people know from experience that it is difficult to have an autonomous sense of self when beholden to others so they urge young people to achieve and maintain financial independence, but many others extended that advice to being personally self reliant in every way.

Seemingly contrary to the admonitions to work with others many people said things like "be independent, don't depend on anyone," "always be your own person," and "decide things for yourself." This seeming contradiction might be resolved by considering that working together is done between well adjusted people who choose to work together rather than being forced by circumstance or expectation. This tempers the possible self centered aspect of advice like "be responsible for yourself," "work it out for yourself," "find your way," and "learn to survive on your own and be self sufficient." But for many people the message seems to be that the best way to live a fulfilling life is to "learn to think for yourself, plan for yourself and stick to your plans, be self-sufficient," and "help yourself and be self-reliant."

This is good advice provided it's done from healthy motivations, but the caution and even bitterness in the advice from some women was unmistakable as older women continued to warn younger women not to be controlled or abused. There were many comments like "keep your independence, especially girls," "don't give yourself to any man, look after yourself and keep your pride and dignity," and "be your own person, always. Women establish your own identity."

"Keep your independence, especially girls."

In a less ominous way, women are encouraged to establish and keep their own identity rather than being a satellite of their husband's personality. "Be your own person as a woman, have power, don't be controlled by a man," "have confidence in yourself and don't be dominated," and "find your goals and determine what you want. You have a choice." And while women are rightly cautioned to be their own person, the overriding point here applies to everyone to "be independent and know what it's like to fend for yourself," "don't let anyone control you," and "be strong in looking after yourself, physically and mentally."

"Be strong in looking after yourself, physically and mentally."

Given the opportunity, older people were eager to pass on advice. Some offered one or two key things but others offered much more including "seek advice from an older, wiser person." Others said "don't be afraid to ask others for opinions," "seek wisdom apart from your own, draw on the wisdom of others," and "listen to advice and learn by good examples."

Contrary to those who encouraged young people to work things out for themselves many others advised them to "get a mentor," "find someone to encourage you and spend time with them," and "have a guide and someone to help you." Many of those interviewed were pleased that this study offered them the chance to speak anonymously to young people and many of them took the opportunity to share their insights encouraging young people to "seek out an elderly person you respect and listen to what they say" and "have a good long talk with an older person about your plans and goals."

"Seek out an elderly person you respect and listen to what they say."

Respect for elders played a big role in much of their thinking as did parental influence. More than a few people said "respect your parents and listen to what they say," and one person said "have good talks with mom or some wiser older person." This was also extended beyond parents as several people also said "talk to your grandparents and senior members of your family to get a sense of your heritage," and "learn about your heritage and know where you come from."

"Learn about your heritage and know where you come from."

The advice presented in this chapter is precisely the kind that they en-

couraged young people to get from older people. This includes perseverance as many older people said "pick something to excel at and persevere."
One person said to remember the PPO principle (perseverance pays off)
and others added "be disciplined in your efforts," "be tenacious," "finish
what you start," and "make up your mind what you want to do and stick to
it." Virtually all older and wiser people understand from experience and
observation that success in any aspect of life does not come without perseverance and tenacity. "Think about what you want to do and push hard to
do it. Persist in doing it. Stay straight and don't let yourself get mastered by
anything."

"Think about what you want to do and push hard to do it."

Being a success at anything in life depends on taking positive steps,
but it also depends on avoiding pitfalls. There were some cautions given to
young people to "be careful, avoid the pitfalls like drugs, booze, cigarettes."
When asked to give advice to young people the first two words out of one
man's mouth were "be sober." Another man said with regret, "don't drink
too much like I did." Others were somewhat softer saying "drink modestly,"
"watch the booze," and "don't drink too much. Alcohol can get you." And
along with the caution to "look after yourself, don't drink or use drugs," was
the warning against smoking. Many older people who either suffered themselves from smoking or watched loved ones suffer warned young people
"don't start smoking," and "I smoked most of my life and have seen the
devastation."

"Don't drink too much like I did."

Along with plenty of good advice and the preceding warnings about
drugs, booze and cigarettes, various warnings both general and specific
were given by many people about other potential pitfalls in life. Typical
of valuable advice from a beloved grandparent people said things like "be
careful about what you enter into, learn what you can, keep your eyes open,"
"be careful and make good judgments," and "be careful where you are and

what you're doing." Such feelings were summed up by one person who said "be careful about the way you live."

More somewhat typical advice about being cautious includes "be careful who you trust," "watch out for con artists and scams," "watch out for people who want to get you or scam you," and "watch out for phony people." And not surprisingly there were warnings about relationships like "avoid unhealthy relationships because you get drawn in," "be careful who you marry," and for girls, "be careful about boys."

"Be careful who you marry."

Amongst the obvious warnings, many people encouraged a heart for giving that makes the world a better place and builds character in the process. This reasoning includes "don't be so focused on yourself, don't think of yourself more than you ought to," "have an outlook to helping others," and "be neighborly." Others elaborated on such thinking saying "give to others always," "give to the poor," and "be there for people when they need you for contentment and hope. Things are hard nowadays."

"Give to others always."

The advice to help others extended to society as one person encouraged young people to "learn to care for others and consider others because our country is democratic politically but not economically. Be politically aware and participate as much as you can." A similar call came from a person who said "be politically and socially active, and have a sense of love that people feel without you speaking about it, thinking love in all you do." Others encouraged young people to "get involved in clubs," and "be interested in world affairs and know what is going on. Follow the news."

"Have a sense of love that people feel without you speaking about it, thinking love in all you do."

Not surprisingly advice was plentiful regarding family and marital is-

sues including making family a priority and keeping the marital relationship happy and healthy. It has been said that marriage is the engine that
drives the family and this was certainly emphasized by those who promoted
healthy marriage as essential to a vibrant family. For most people this begins with a proper "attitude toward relationship and commitment," to "stay
married." One person wisely said "work at your relationship and work on
yourself, be friends with your partner," and another added "work on your
marriage to keep it vibrant." Several people referred to "communication
in marriage," and the most pointed advice came from a person who said
"respect the institution of marriage and ask, 'What can I give?' rather than,
'What can I get?'"

"Work on your marriage to keep it vibrant."

More advice included "work together with your partner," and "don't try
to change your prospective mate and don't let him change you." Others were
adamant that young people should "have a mutually respectful and equal relationship," as older women said to young men "treat your wife as an equal,"
and young women "trust and believe your husband."

"Have a mutually respectful and equal relationship."

Beyond relationship issues of mutual respect many others offered specific
advice from their own experience like "don't bring up your mate's faults in
front of other people," "don't go to sleep angry with your mate," and "don't
walk out when you have an argument."

After espousing the benefits of a healthy, happy marriage, many people
spoke of recognizing the importance of family. Several people said to "get
married and have your kids younger. Don't start too late." One person felt
the need to make a case for even having kids in the modern world saying "a
child is much better than a pet. Many people have replaced kids with pets."
But many others spoke fondly of having more children encouraging young
people to "have more than one child if you can, raising a family is a joy,"
"have a larger family, have them when you're young," and "enjoy your kids

because they grow up fast."

"Enjoy your kids because they grow up fast."

Appeal to traditional values continued as people said things like "be faithful to your family," "work with your spouse to build a life together raising kids," and "take full responsibility for your kids. Show them hard work and have fun when you work." Older women continued to speak to younger women saying "dedicate your lives to raising children," and "be devoted to your husband, kids, job, etc. Devotion is key in all things." The overriding point from most everyone was to "create a good and healthy family environment for your kids." Family values were paramount for most saying things like "invest yourself in your children and put them before your own stuff," "spend time with your kids and make them important in your life," "listen to your kids," and "discipline your kids." Discipline was an important issue for many who gave advice like "be equal and consistent parents," and "teach them properly to be kind and honest." One kind man said to remember that "a mile and a smile go a long way in disciplining a child," a pleasant walk to talk things over.

"A mile and a smile go a long way in disciplining a child."

But not every approach was quite as gentle as one person said "start thinking about money issues and teach your children that lesson. You only get what you work for so don't make it too easy for your kids." But just as quickly the onus was put back on the parents as one person warned "don't club your kids to death (skating, bowling, etc), spend time with them," "teach your kids to appreciate the simple things," and "raise your kids to be independent and self reliant."

"You only get what you work for so don't make it too easy for your kids."

A great deal of advice was offered on what is most important in life, and many older people encouraged young people to resist the temptation to focus on material things and to be thankful for what they have. It was not lost on those interviewed that the present generation has much more than the previous one and faces the danger of becoming fixated on material possessions. This prompted comments like "don't be envious or you'll never be content, accept that you can't have everything," "material things are not that important," "don't be so focused on material things" and "do some soul searching."

The point they all seemed to want to make is "try to enjoy simpler things in life, less TV and computer," and "don't just pursue money and things. Rather, pursue contentment." Perhaps the most profound response that best captured this sentiment came from a man who said "try to shrink the difference between what you want and what you have."

"Try to shrink the difference between what you want and what you have."

Closely related to the foregoing warning against materialism was the advice for young people to "learn to give thanks for things." Several people said to young people "be grateful and have an attitude of gratitude," and "look at what you have rather than what you don't have and appreciate what you have." Some even brought attention to the sacrifice of the previous generation that led to the current prosperity saying "learn about history and how hard people worked to give you opportunity," "don't waste money," and "don't be wasteful." One person simply said "make the best of where you're at, and whatever your circumstance, be thankful." Another summed up the overall sentiment saying "be happy with what you have so don't just pursue money and things. Rather pursue contentment and be thankful."

"Be grateful and have an attitude of gratitude."

Along the same lines and typical of the generation interviewed many people made comments we've all heard before like "try to behave," "respect your elders," and "respect your parents and authority." This is perhaps the closest thing to finger wagging heard so far, but this practical advice rein-forced the point of building character through respect for elders, laws and authority.

Beyond that, it was about helping to sustain the systems that bring or-der to our lives and allow us to succeed in family and society. A further practical aspect concerned the negative drain on a person's success fighting authority. It becomes a stumbling block to success fighting battles that don't need to be fought and can't be won. That is the practical side of the advice to "keep on straight and narrow, resist temptations of the modern world," and "learn to follow rules and respect authority."

More positive advice continued from older people who said "enjoy your life." Many had been so caught up in the difficulties and hard work that looking back realized they forgot to try to enjoy the process. Recall that many people had little or no holiday time due to work and financial pres-sure. This prompted many to say "take life as it comes and try to enjoy the process," "have fun, pay yourself first," and "balance work and play. Work hard but take time to enjoy."

"Balance work and play. Work hard but take time to enjoy."

There is no doubt that it is difficult for many people who have a well de-veloped work ethic and enjoy working hard to slow down and enjoy life. As a result there is little value seen in down time. But most of those who lived this pattern and looked back said "balance work with relaxation time." This is the result of the perspective change from looking ahead when life seems long and full of opportunity to looking back when it seems short and full of hard work with little relaxation time. This prompted many to say "enjoy your life because it might be short." One widow said "enjoy life because it's too darn short. You marry a guy one day and bury him the next." The best representation of this mindset came from a man who said "enjoy life. This is not a rehearsal. Don't sweat the small stuff."

"Enjoy life. This is not a rehearsal. Don't sweat the small stuff."

Many people from the generation interviewed sacrificed their body to a combination of hard work, lack of exercise, poor eating habits, alcohol, smoking, and lack of medical and dental attention. The resulting regret caused many to say things like "take care of your body, it's the only one you've got," and "look after your health. Don't abuse your body because you'll need it." Many people had dental problems and even lost their teeth later in life prompting one person to say "take care of your teeth; do it now because there are always reasons not to do things." The overall message from people who had learned the hard way was to "exercise and stay physically fit," "do things," "eat right," and "join the gym."

"Take care of your body; it's the only one you've got."

Along the same lines of staying physically (and mentally) fit was the advice from many to get involved in sports, drama and music. Because this caused regret for so many people, it's not surprising that many older people who felt they had missed out on such things due to work and responsibility urged young people to "seek sports and competition," "take music lessons," and "take up music for its beauty, and love the arts."

Others wanted to encourage young people to "travel all you can and obtain all the knowledge you can, new people, new customs, different perspectives," as well as "other cultures and languages."

According to those interviewed another important element in living a happy, healthy and meaningful life is learning to get along well with people which involves the ability to listen and show patience, tolerance and understanding. We all remember a grandparent who said "you have two ears and one mouth" so "listen rather than talk." "If you're silent you learn more than when you're talking," "so listen to others and learn from them."

Similar advice continued as people speaking from experience said things like "be tolerant and understanding, listen and understand, and show patience. Somebody may be right, not me. Don't be narrow-minded," "learn how to communicate with people," and "be reasonable with people." Regrets led many people to the understanding that we need to "compromise with others and nothing is cut and dry." Such realization also caused many to advise against the closed minded attitude that typified many people of the older generation eliciting comments like "be open-minded about race, religion, nationalities," and "keep an open mind to other cultures, ideas, and politics." This was capped off by typical but timeless advice, "don't be so self centered and know it all. "

"Be tolerant and understanding, listen & understand."

Another common caution we've all heard from older people has to do with friends. Many parents have said "avoid the wrong crowd," "pick good friends, bring good people into your life," and "keep good company, friends, family, upstanding people." With that in mind older people said things like "have lots of friends," "be true to your friends, and "value and trust your friends."

"Bring good people into your life."

One of the least said but most valuable pieces of advice was to "maintain your sense of humor all your life," and "laugh a lot." Some were able to do that but most seemed to see the value in it only after the fact but were too caught up with life's pressure to have lived it. Having said that, however, lots of people enjoyed a laugh and some were even funny without necessarily trying to be. One woman advised younger women "don't give too much easy sex," while another wanted to say to them "men are little boys grown up, and I love it." In looking at life's issues one man advised younger men to "have a beer or half a dozen beer, lots of beer." He was from the old school of "let's have a drink and think about it."

"Maintain your sense of humor all your life."

Maintaining the kind of balance spelled out in this chapter is no doubt difficult, some might say impossible. But it's something to strive for. In many ways this chapter is a blueprint for a prosperous and happy life provided by those who either achieved one or learned by experience what it takes to create one. The practical knowledge it contains would help anyone find a measure of contentment and that is most certainly their wish for you, to go well and find your peace. Remember the words above to "find contentment however you can," and "make the most of your life" because "this is not a rehearsal."

"Find contentment however you can."

CHAPTER 9

GROWING OLD

AS WE AGE WE CHANGE, our body, our perspective, and our understanding, and presumably we become wiser. So given that I was asking people for their wisdom based on age and experience I wanted to get a sense of how they understand and deal with the process of ageing.

It's a symptom of old age that some people become less tolerant and more irritable, and everyone knows an older person who is grumpy. But it also seems that many older people mellow with age and become nicer as they are released from many of the pressures of daily life. I was curious how older people view this and see themselves.

Before asking about being grumpy I first asked about patience, "Are you more patient now you're older or less patient?" Fifty-six percent said they are more patient, eleven percent said they are less patient, thirty percent said about the same as always (either patient or impatient) and three percent couldn't decide so said fifty-fifty.

MORE OR LESS PATIENT?
▌ 56% - more
▌ 11% - less
▌ 30% - same
▌ 3% - not sure

It is a reasonable assumption that people mellow with age, and that was the case for most people in this survey who said things like "I had no patience when I was young but have mellowed with age," "I used to have a short fuse," and "impatience gets you nowhere." Others had more specific reasons for becoming more patient like "I can give my grandkids the love I didn't give my own kids," "I'm a deeply religious person," and "I read Seneca and adopted Stoicism." Resignation seemed to bring more patience as well from people who have lost much of their fight and said "I surrender all," or "I'm just tired."

"I had no patience when I was young but have mellowed with age."

Those who were more impatient were aware of it and tended to admit their short coming directly offering answers like "I'm not more patient, and I wish I had more patience earlier," and "I've always been impatient but even less now." Others offered justifications for their increased lack of patience like "I'm less patient because of illness," "I'm less patient living with my own dissatisfaction and feeling I could have done better," and "I'm less patient with myself but more patient with others and other things." One lady admitted "I'm less patient now because I'm old fashioned and expect values like giving an elder a seat."

"I've always been impatient but even less now."

Those who said they are the same as always said things like "I've always been patient and still am," "I've always been an even tempered person," and "I'm a very mellow person." The best response came from a man who just smirked and said "I'm Joe cool."

"I've always been an even tempered person."

Most of those who admitted to having a more impatient nature and remained the same throughout their lives were surprisingly unapologetic and actually quite charming. A few people said "I'm not patient now and never was," and another said "I'm the same, Irish temper." I realized that it is possible for people to describe themselves as impatient yet be quite pleasant and likeable. Also, impatience is distinct from grumpiness.

"I'm not patient now and never was."

Eighty-two percent of those interviewed described themselves as happy, fifteen percent answered fifty-fifty and only three percent admitted to being grumpy. Very few people were willing to describe themselves as grumpy, but there were those who did admit that they are "sometimes grumpy," and one person admitted with a chuckle that "others think so," which is perhaps more revealing than any self assessment. For most others their admission was qualified in some way offering reasons like "I'm happy as long as no-body bugs me," and "I'm not grumpy, just lonely."

"I'm happy as long as nobody bugs me."

Some were hesitant to admit being grumpy but too honest to say they weren't so those who answered fifty-fifty about whether they are grumpy offered reasons like "being in a wheelchair," "my eyesight is so bad that I'm frustrated," or other reasons related to being incapacitated or in discomfort in some way due to age or illness. One person shared his struggle saying "I'm staying level, but it is an issue."

"I'm staying level, but it is an issue."

The overwhelming majority of people were admittedly happy and more than willing to elaborate saying things like "I'm very positive," "I don't know what it is to be grumpy," and "I've hardly ever been upset. My dad was like that." Others gave examples like "I sing a lot," "I'm a merry widow not a black widow," and "I purpose to be one of God's children, kind, pa-tient, trustworthy, and pleasant."

"I don't know what it is to be grumpy."

I was also curious how much and how often people reflect on their younger lives so I asked, "Do you remember your youth often?" Fifteen percent said no, thirteen percent said sometimes and seventy-two percent said yes. Those who said no were usually quite direct saying things like "it wasn't pleasant," "I've forgotten a lot of stuff," and "I live in the present and future." More specific responses include "I worked all the time on the farm," "not really, a lot of tough times as a war child in England"(several people said this), and "I take one day at a time."

The fifty-fifty responses were similar to those who said no and were almost always qualified in some way with explanations like "I remember the good times," and "some bad times in childhood and some good times in my twenties."

Many of those who answered yes about remembering their younger years usually smiled and offered responses like "even more so now," "it was good," and "fondly." Many people reflected on their younger years saying things like "when I was young and free," "I danced a lot," and "we played board games."

But of those who said they remember their youth often it wasn't all pleasant reflection as others said things like "I had a bad time as a child, war years, hunger, parents fighting, then bad marriages," "I often wonder where the boys from the orphanage are," and "yes, but only earlier parts because I'm losing my memories now."

Life goes through many stages and it seems that one's best years would be somewhere before old age, maybe childhood, the young adult years, the years with young children, the career years, or perhaps the early retirement years. Because of this it also seems that many people would spend their latter years reliving those best years through memories and stories. This would especially be the case in advanced years when a spouse and friends have died, children have moved on and the work days are long since finished. So when I asked people directly whether they live in the past, I was surprised that only six percent said yes, fifteen percent said fifty-fifty and an overwhelming seventy-nine percent said no, and most of those were emphatic.

Those who admitted to living in the past were reticent to do so and generally spoke with resignation accepting it like a defeat as one lady hung her head and said "my parents are gone, husband gone, and most brothers and sisters gone." But most people didn't outright admit living in the past so answered fifty-fifty and gave responses like "for the most part," and "sometimes, but I know I have to live in the present." Of living in the past one person said "I desperately try not to." For others it was all about missing people who are gone like one man who pined for his second wife or a lady who said "I miss my husband terribly." A ninety-six year old man who answered fifty-fifty admitted "all I have left is memories."

"All I have left is memories."

But these were by no means typical answers as many people of advanced age were adamant that they live in the present. Positive responses include "I don't wish for yesterday at all," "I live one day at a time," and "I live right in the present." Some even scolded others for living in the past saying "too many people do that," and "we must always look to the future." One person quoted the often heard cliché "yesterday is history, tomorrow is a mystery, today is a gift, this moment is mine." Others were respectful of the past saying "I remember it fondly," and one person who insisted she doesn't live in the past said "I say to people I wish you had the life we had."

"I live right in the present."

The next question was whether people still feel young at heart and the answers were even more surprising than the previous one as only two percent said no with comments like "I'd just as soon lie in bed," and "I'm ready to go." Ten percent said fifty-fifty offering comments like "I try to," and "I try. Every day is different."

The overwhelming majority of answers were positive and upbeat as a surprising eighty-eight percent of people were adamant that they feel young at heart. They expressed their views on ageing with comments like "yes, I am young," "I don't even think of age," "age is only a number," and "I don't feel any different." Others were inspired saying "I'm only sixteen inside, when I look in the mirror I don't recognize the person," and "despite ageing, the world still looks the same from inside."

"Despite ageing, the world still looks the same from inside."

For others their youth was exemplified in the way they look at themselves and things they still like to do prompting responses like "I'm still crazy," "I'm up at 5:30 every day," and "I love to go places and do things." One lady laughingly said "I could dance all night." It was apparent that being young at heart is primarily about attitude and most people were committed to staying that way as revealed in such comments as "I still need a challenge all the time," and "I like to have something to look forward to every day. I like to accomplish something every day no matter how small."

"I'm still crazy."

As for engaging the modern world, I was curious how many older people owned a computer, were online or had a cellular phone. The numbers were relatively even in this regard as forty-three percent owned a computer while fifty-seven percent did not and thirty-nine percent were online while sixty-one percent were not. Thirty-nine percent owned a cell phone while sixty-one percent did not. The determining factors were cost, necessity, attitude and interest. Some people said they could never justify the expense of such things, some had no need for such devices, others didn't think they could understand how to use them, and many others were just disinterested. Conversely, many others had the interest and were fully engaged in the modern world of computers and cell phones. Some even had more than one computer.

TOP TEN ANSWERS
TO THE BEST PART OF GROWING OLD
1. Freedom, more time to do what I want, social events, travel, etc
2. Still relatively healthy and active
3. Content and enjoying my life
4. Less pressure, responsibility, worry, anxiety and concern
5. Financial Stability / Pension
6. No Best Part
7. Doing Lots, Staying Busy, Hobbies
8. Retirement, not having to work
9. Family, kids, grandkids
10. Wiser, learned a lot

When asked "What's the best part of growing old?" the overwhelming majority of people responded right away with one word "freedom." For most this meant "I'm not on the clock," "I can do whatever I want," and "I'm completely independent, physically and financially." I also discovered that most seniors have a well developed social network and are very active in many ways with games, events, travel, etc. One lady put it best when she said "every day is Sunday."

"Every day is Sunday."

The second most popular response was that many seniors appreciate being relatively healthy and still able to do things. Responses include "not being ill," "good health," and "I'm still healthy, my mind is clear and I'm thin and in good shape." Others were upbeat saying "I've been very healthy except for eyesight," and "I've smoked for seventy-three years and have great lungs. I'm very healthy overall."

"I'm still healthy, my mind is clear and I'm thin and in good shape."

Despite the aches and pains of growing old and the inevitable illness that comes with age, a surprising number of seniors felt very healthy and many related their view of age saying things like "I feel great, feel young, think young, I'm very healthy," "I feel way younger than I am, the outside does not mesh with the inside," and "I don't see myself as old and don't look in the mirror much." One impressive lady who was well in to her eighties asked, "If you didn't know how old you are how old would you be?" This thinking was exemplified by a man who said "I feel the same even though I'm one hundred. I'm healthy, my mind is good, and I have good blood circulation." Another person summed up the sentiment by saying "I'm thankful every day I'm here. I can still do things."

"If you didn't know how old you are how old would you be?"

Next in most popular responses were those who said they are content and enjoying life. Inspiring answers include "I'm more content and live each day as it comes," "I just enjoy the age I am and live in the moment," and "I have a sense of calm and tranquility." One person said "I'm ageing gracefully and have no regrets." Many of the responses to this question were an inspiration for people of any age with comments like "I'm content and easy to please," "I'm more tolerant and learning to enjoy things," and "I've accomplished lots and feel good." Contentment was self evident with comments like "life as a whole has been good," "I'm happy within myself," and "I'm happy with my life the way it is."

"I just enjoy the age I am and live in the moment."

More comments on the enjoyment of old age include "I'm getting lazier, I worked very hard all my life," and "I enjoy sleeping in." There was a real sense from most of these people that after hardship, work and life difficulties they were able to find some enjoyment in their latter years saying things like "I appreciate each day and am youthful in my thinking," and "I'm living the life I want." Others elaborated saying "I'm the same person I was when I was younger, I was always a fun person," "I'm having a ball, can come and go as I please," and "I feel like I'm really living my life now." These comments sound like a party when strung together and one person added "I'm never going to grow up."

"I'm never going to grow up."

Several comments reflect more of a balance between contentment and enjoyment with those who said "I'm appreciating life and how lucky I've been," "every day is a new day," and "I'm always singing and whistling. I love music and staying with people my own age. I can relate to them." One lady was content "finding serenity and peace after difficulties, accepting people the way they are and feeling content that I don't have to change them. I don't have to like them but I have to love them." A similar response came from a person who said "I appreciate life more. I have survived colon cancer. I see the important things more. I appreciate my gifts and can share them with the world."

"I appreciate my gifts and can share them with the world."

Many people were positive about old age because of less pressure, responsibility, worry and the anxiety of their working years and caring for a family. Answering instantly one person said the best part of ageing is "less pressure, I accept things easier," and another added "less anxiety and fear, less concerned about things." One lady half jokingly said "freedom from dishes, kids, cooking, shopping, work, responsibilities," and in a similar way a man said "I can't get laid off."

This was tied closely to financial stability and pensions as many people were quick to say that they are happy "knowing that the bills are paid" and "not worrying about money." Others said things like "life is easier now, I have a pension," and "you get paychecks without working and have financial peace of mind."

"You get paychecks without working."

Of all the positive responses to the best part of growing old, there were also many who gave various negative responses saying there is no best part. One person simply said "I hate it, but accept it," and another said "there's no choice in the matter so just do the best you can to be nice." It seems that bitterness emerged for some who either didn't want old age or it wasn't what they had expected it to be. One person remarked "there are no golden years, just rusty," and another said of old age "there's nothing good about it. It's for the birds." Such attitudes were perhaps due to the frustration of loss of family and friends, illness or feeling less important, as indicated by a person who said of old age "I'm not doing as much useful stuff."

"There are no golden years, just rusty."

But for any who were negative and felt less useful, there were many more who said the opposite that in their golden years they are doing lots, staying busy and have lots of hobbies. Some were even still working in to their eighties. Such attitudes are reflected in comments like "I'm still very engaged in lots of stuff," "busier than ever, doing what I want," and "still totally involved in life every day, work, family, business, etc."

"Still totally involved in life every day."

For others retirement was the chance to enjoy life and not have to go to work, and that was amongst the most popular responses. The pressure of work was obviously taxing for some people who gave responses like "I've done my life work and can relax a bit without the world hanging on my actions," and "I don't have to run my own business anymore. I was a slave to it." For others it was specific aspects of their job they were happy to leave behind like not having to work in the winter, not having to commute in rush hour traffic, and for one relieved soul "no more meetings."

"I've done my life work and can relax a bit."

Less time at work means more time with family and many people were only too happy to express that as one of the joys of old age. For one lady it was "spending more time with my husband," but for most others it was children and grand children that brought a smile. One person said "I get to see my family more often," and another added "I enjoy seeing my children's lives, and grandchildren, and being included in their lives." Others took personal satisfaction in "watching the family grow," and "seeing the achievements of my kids." For at least one person it was mutual saying "I help my kids and they help me."

"I enjoy seeing my children's lives, and grandchildren, and being included in their lives."

Along with some satisfaction in advanced years many people were happy to acknowledge and appreciate the wisdom and experience that comes with age and could say it as a fact rather than a boast. One person said with humility "with age comes wisdom. I'm getting some sense in my head. I've learned some things." A person spoke of his "wisdom, knowledge, and contentment," while another spoke of "wisdom and knowledge," saying "I'm satisfied with my life."

"With age comes wisdom. I'm getting some sense in my head."

Several people spoke in practical terms about being smarter with age and appreciating the knowledge they have accumulated, drawing from their experiences, and being able to do lots of things. But for most the focus was on wisdom. One person said "I'm wiser now, even though it's too late." He openly wished he had been wiser earlier in life, wise beyond his years, and could have had at least some of the understanding then that he gained later. Several comments exemplify this thinking and include "I have a better understanding and I'm at peace," "I have a greater understanding of God and how the world works," "I realize that the world is a picture and that life around me matters," and "I understand what's important in life and can see the beauty in life."

"I have a better understanding and I'm at peace."

For many people the beauty in life involved "gaining lots of friends" and relating to other people. Another person took some comfort in the fact that "other people are getting older too. I've got friends my own age." It eases the sting of old age knowing that you're not alone and that it is part of a bigger picture that everyone must endure. Another person spoke of her "nice neighbors who care for each other more." Many people expressed something similar to this in that older people who have endured life's battles and trials tend to be nicer to one another. Their spirit softens with age.

"Other people are getting older too. I've got friends my own age."

This is perhaps in part due to the wisdom that age brings but many older people also expressed having more confidence and a better sense of self. For one person the best part of growing old is "being who I am the way that I am." A surprising number of people made similar statements saying things like "I'm much more my own person now," "more calm and assured about things," and "have more confidence and wisdom." Others said things like "I'm not so competitive now, I am my own person," "I can talk to young men, they open the door for me, and I'm not as self conscious." Another added that as an older person "you can say what you want and wear what you want."

"I'm much more my own person now."

The thrust of what they were saying is that contentment comes in some measure when life's battles have largely been settled and a strong sense of self is firmly established. There is no one left to impress, no competition looming and much less responsibility and stress. As one person put it, this is the time when "you can be at peace with yourself," and another added "people can't push you around; you have a better sense of self and only have to worry about yourself." It is this kind of understanding that prompted one person to say the best part of growing old is "being able to live by myself and enjoy my own company."

"Being able to live by myself and enjoy my own company."

Living in a comfortable place brought lots of joy for people in their advanced years and many people spoke very fondly of their living arrangement, either their own home, a comfortable apartment, an in-law suite, or assisted living. One couple said they were honored to live in a suite with their son and family, and many others were happy to live in an in-law suite in their children's home. Others had their apartment arranged with furniture, trinkets and pictures from the past in a way that made them comfortable.

Some said the best part of growing old is "living in an assisted living home," "being in my care home," and "being in a comfortable, happy environment." Those who had worked hard all their lives serving others and meeting responsibilities especially appreciated the assisted living and acted almost surprised saying "everything is done for me," "it's like living in a luxury hotel," and "I like living at my care home." I asked almost everyone I interviewed in a care home whether or not they were happy and most said yes.

Funny answers to the question about the best part of growing old include "just being alive," "being able to get up in the morning and say hi," and "waking up in the morning and not seeing my name in the obituary column of the newspaper." It was somewhat tongue in cheek but also a serious answer as several people said the best part of growing old is "I'm still alive," "life itself, just living my life," and "getting here without dying." Others added "I'm thankful every day I'm here," and "I feel lucky to even be alive at ninety-two." Many were lighthearted about age saying "I live one day at a time. I wake up in the morning and pinch myself and if it hurts I say 'Good Morning' and get moving."

"I'm thankful every day I'm here."

One of the best parts of ageing for many people is happy memories, and, according to one person, "being able to review my life." Several people spoke about feeling blessed, having time to enjoy life and then being lucky enough to look back on it fondly. One person said the best part of growing old is "looking back on my accomplishments and all the things I did," and for another it is "remembering a happy marriage." Many widows and widowers reflected on the past with their spouse and reminisced of a time when things were good.

As people continued to give many and varied responses to the best part of growing old it was sometimes surprising what they think is important. Several seniors expressed appreciation at the respect they receive because of their elder status with comments like "people open doors for me." Others enjoy benefits at stores and restaurants, and for one person it is Seniors Wednesdays at IHOP (International House of Pancakes).

Several people have appreciated the opportunity in their old age to mature in their faith and establish a greater peace with God. One person was pleased to have "much more time for prayer and meditation," and another pointed to faith and "knowing it's not over when I die." And it seems odd but for some people a positive part of ageing is about looking toward the end and dying. One person said he appreciates "having time to prepare for eventual sickness and death," another said that the nice thing about old age is "you don't have to face it too long," and for another it was "looking forward to going to heaven."

There were many comical things said, some intentionally and some not, but humor played a role for many people as one person said about life "I've covered a lot of ground, come a long way, and developed a good sense of humor along the way." Another pragmatic person simply said "laughing is better than crying. Crying never gets you anywhere." One man said he is happy because "I don't have to be around complaining women all the time," and another said "the way the world is going, I'm glad I'm going out of it rather than into it."

TOP TEN ANSWERS
TO THE WORST PART OF GROWING OLD.

- 1. Aches and Pains, Physical limitations, Lack of energy
- 2. Being inactive, Can't get out and do as much like travel and activities
- 3. Nothing, No worst part
- 4. Serious Illness, cancer, stroke, etc
- 5. Loss of Family and Friends
- 6. Loneliness and depression
- 7. Loss of Independence, Being a Burden, Needing Care
- 8. Looking ahead to Illness and Death
- 9. Getting old and wanting to be younger
- 10. Loss of memory and brain functioning

The overwhelming majority of people interviewed said that the worst part of growing old is the aches and pains. They didn't elaborate much but just spoke about age related health issues, physical limitations, and lack of energy. One person summed it saying "every day something hurts."

"Every day something hurts."

The second most common age related complaint was inactivity and not being able to do as many things as before. There were various reasons for this such as lack of mobility, desire, or resources. One person said he had a difficult time "giving things up," and another said he "would have liked to work longer" and as a result doesn't have enough challenges. Due to the often more restricted circumstance of the retired lifestyle one person said "sometimes I get bored." Others said things like "I'm getting lazier,""I procrastinate more being inactive," and "I can't travel as much now that I'm widowed."

Because of all the positive responses to getting old it is perhaps not surprising that many people answered the question about the worst part of growing old in a positive way. They were so focused on being upbeat they wouldn't acknowledge any down side and offered responses like "just take life as it comes," "it's just what you make of it," and "just get old gracefully." Acceptance was again a key idea as people made comments like "I accept what will be," "I just carry on and do my best," and "I don't even worry about it. We all have our time." One lady who had suffered terribly along with her children at the hand of an abusive, alcoholic husband was finally at peace and living in comfort in her later years. When asked about the worst part of being old she just laughed and said "I love being old."

"I love being old."

Virtually everyone who suffered a serious illness such as cancer, stroke, heart disease, lung disease, or other severely debilitating conditions named it as the worst part of growing old. One lady had a stroke which caused her to be in a wheelchair and severely diminished her quality of life. Several others had lung disease and breathing problems from smoking. One lady in a care facility responded by saying "I've had kidney problems, heart attack, blocked arteries, enzyme problems, hips replaced, and I can't breathe. I went from being healthy and active to being incapacitated in a short period of time." Another person said "I can't drive, am dying of cancer and have had to give up a lot of things."

"I just carry on and do my best."

Blindness was a serious issue for several people and was a life chang-ing event that brought about great frustration. One lady began going blind in her sixties and is now unable to participate in games, go out very much or interact with others. She is relegated to one room and her talking books for the most part of every day. I was so affected by her that I went to visit her twice and promised to make this work into a talking book for her and everyone in her position.

Not surprisingly the loss of family and friends was for many the worst part of growing old. Many people interviewed had lost a spouse and made comments like "I didn't have the chance to retire with my wife as we planned," "my plans all changed when my husband died," and "retirement was good but my husband died." Others who lost family said "I'm the last of all my family to still be alive," and "most of my family is dead, wife, son, siblings, mom, dad." For others it was "friends dying around you and the realization that your turn is coming." One man said "it sounds strange but I was trying to get a passport signed and had difficulty finding people who have known me for two years or more because most of them are dead."

"I'm the last of all my family to still be alive."

It's a sad fact that many older people suffer from loneliness and many made comments like "loneliness is really hard," "I'm very sad at times and lonely," and "loneliness, my wife still lives at home and I live here in a care home." Others elaborated on their difficulty "being a widow and alone, husband died fourteen months ago," "depression since my wife died," and one person said "I'm very alone, last brother died two years ago." One lady shared her struggle dealing with her husband's death saying "I've lost what I've lived for all my life," and another described the worst part of grow-ing old saying "we always had a big house, music, and people. I went from Grand Central Station to the morgue, living alone."

"I'm very sad at times and lonely."

Living arrangements and lack of ability were an issue for many people as some complained of losing their independence and being a burden to others. One person said the worst part about getting older is "you can't do things for yourself. Being dependent is hard because I was always so independent." For others it was "always asking people to do things for me," "can't do things when there's work to be done," and "being a burden to family" but "don't want to impose."

"Being dependent is hard because I was always so independent."

Receiving care made many people more comfortable, and there is no doubt they appreciated it, but for many others it was swallowing their pride to be receiving assistance after a lifetime of giving assistance. When asked about the worst part of growing old a former teacher and man in his nineties looked at me and asked if I really wanted to know, honestly. After telling him I did, he quietly said "losing bowel control; it's embarrassing."

Many people spoke about the joy of living in a care home as one of the best parts of growing old, feeling secure and looked after, but for many others it was the opposite and not where they wanted to be as it created restrictions that come with age along with lack of mobility and resources. One person voiced her dissatisfaction of "not living in my own home, not as mobile as I used to be and no car." For many people losing their driver's license and car was a significant life change and difficult adjustment. Others spoke of the frustration of "living in a care home," with some saying "I can't go out on my own." One lady who had travelled extensively and lived a full life simply said "my world is closed in now to one room."

"My world is closed in now to one room."

Similar resignation was expressed by many people who were looking ahead to illness and death, "looking at the end," "knowing you're going to die," and "waiting to pass on." Some used the analogy of the hourglass running out, and time had obviously become a stark reality for those who made comments like "I realize that there's more behind me than ahead," "there's so much more I want to do but won't live long enough to do it," and "I'm wondering how much time I have left." It had become difficult for some living with the "impending sense that I'm not going to be here for much longer."

"There's so much more I want to do
but won't live long enough to do it."

Some people just named old age itself as the worst part of growing old with responses like "growing old," "being old," and "getting old; I refuse to get old." This sentiment was expressed by a lady who said "old age snuck up on me and my hair went gray," and another who said "I don't like the idea of being a feeble old person struggling with age." For most it was a reference to wishing they had more time and were young again with comments like "I'd like to live another forty years," "I'm not twenty anymore, I'd love to be reincarnated," and "I'd like to stay young but I can't live forever so learn to accept it."

"I'd like to stay young but I can't live forever
so learn to accept it."

Loss of memory and brain functioning were difficult for some and several people joked about "senior's moments." But it was more serious than that for most with comments like "I'm forgetful much more," "I can't remember as much so I do some dumb things," and "I can't balance as many things because my capability is diminished somewhat." Pride and frustration were unmistakable as people made comments like "I can't spell as well as I used to," and "I used to be sharp but now can't even speak properly."

"I used to be sharp but now can't even speak properly."

It was these kinds of frustrations that made many older people feel marginalized. One lady said the worst part for her is "people thinking you can't do things," and others said "I don't feel needed as much," and "I don't want to be marginalized just because I can't do all the things I used to." Several others elaborated on similar feelings with one person saying "I can't read because I can't see properly and I can't do as much as I used to, cooking, working, etc. It affects your sense of self, purpose, worth, ability, and confidence. I'm not as outgoing now. I feel like a little old lady which I don't like." One lady living in a care facility said with resignation "it was hard when I came to the realization that I'm not the most important person in anyone's life anymore; my husband died and the kids are all gone."

> *"It was hard when I came to the realization that I'm not the most important person in anyone's life anymore; my husband died and the kids are all gone."*

Such feelings caused one person to say "I've lost my identity a bit and feel out of touch." And for another the worst part is "being referred to as an 'old person,' other people's perspective of you, and people's attitude toward you." One lady spoke of ageism with acceptance saying "I don't think young people see me at all, you become invisible," and another added, "young people don't even notice I'm alive." Such feelings elicited comments like "I'm falling behind because of my age. The world is passing me by." Others said the worst part of ageing is "changing your ways and watching the world change around you," and "realizing life is passing you by."

> *"I don't think young people see me at all. You become invisible."*

Others were frustrated by old age because of financial reasons like not having a pension or enough savings. For one person this meant being "house rich and cash poor," and another who lacked money was "disappointed with forced retirement and couldn't find work after."

Adding to all the difficulties of ageing were the visual effects. Recall the woman who told me she used to be very attractive. For her and others looking in the mirror has become more difficult with advanced age. Some made comments like "appearance," "wrinkling up," and "seeing your body decaying." One lady said "I'm shocked when I look in the mirror to see the little old lady. Old age has caught up to me and I'm feeling my age." Others said things like "I don't recognize the person I see in the mirror," and "I feel the same from the inside but don't look the same on the outside."

"I feel the same from the inside but don't look the same on the outside."

Some people were frustrated with ageing to the point that they wanted it to end. One person half jokingly said the worst part about growing old is "still being alive." The feelings speak for themselves as people made comments like "I don't want to live very long, I just want to die, I have too much pain and am just putting in time, I don't think people should live so long, nothing works right and you're just like a rusty, broken down old car." Similar comments include "I don't want to live too long, I can hardly walk and can't look after myself like I could," and "I've lost my wife and have physical problems, I'm running out. The sooner I'm dead the better. I'm doomed." One man who was once proud but now defeated said "I'm no good to anyone and waiting to go. I'm just here waiting to die. I'm past my expiry date."

"I don't think people should live so long, nothing works right and you're just like a rusty, broken down old car."

Others continued to share age related frustrations like struggling with the illness of loved ones, gaining weight because of eating more, exercising less, and slowing down. Still others had difficulty living with regrets from the past and, as one person put it, "looking back on things I wish I had done."

The worst part of growing old for many people is fear, fear of death, incapacitation, loneliness, and many other things. Several people said "I dread being incapacitated," and another had a "fear of being completely alone." One man simply said "I'm getting older and scared I'm going to die."

"I'm getting older and scared I'm going to die."

TOP TEN ANSWERS TO, "HOW DO YOU MINIMIZE THE WORST PARTS OF GROWING OLD?"

- 1. Stay Busy / hobbies / social activities, etc
- 2. Family and friends
- 3. Stay Positive and mentally tough
- 4. Acceptance, Take Life as it Comes
- 5. Help others, Volunteer
- 6. Faith / Church / Prayer
- 7. Medication to Control things
- 8. Try to Stay Healthy
- 9. Laughing / Sense of Humor
- 10. Live in the Present and Be Thankful

With all the negative responses in the previous section, it was important for me to ask how people cope with such struggles without wallowing into depression. This section in many ways mirrors the section on the best parts of growing old as many people were surprisingly positive and willing to share the ways they deal with their difficulties. I wanted direct answers in dealing with the difficulties of ageing, but in many ways these answers are a good blueprint for anyone dealing with difficulty.

For most people, coping with age related difficulties was helped greatly by having something to do, some reason to go on, and some way to relate to others in a meaningful and positive way. One person found it important "to have challenges I can meet." For others it was important to "stay busy, keep active," "accomplish something," and "keep on doing the things I'm doing as long as I live." Even the one loner in the bunch who didn't find comfort in the company of others said "I'm a loner so I read a lot and ride on my scooter."

Quite a few people mentioned the importance of having some kind of routine like one person who said "I plan my day, stay in touch with friends, read, and go to social events." Others said things like "I get out of the house, attend social clubs, find people I can talk to," "I'm up at seven and plan my day, have lots to do, lots of friends," and "I stay very busy, have a full calendar and get involved in things." One inspiring person said "at eighty-five years old there's so much yet that we can do," and another said "I can't sit still. I'm fully engaged in everything, hobbies, swimming, playing piano, sewing, knitting."

"I stay very busy have a full calendar and get involved in things."

There were many comments about finding comfort in relationships as people spoke of "having lots of good friends, meeting new friends, being neighborly and spending time enjoying family." One person said that it's important to "meet new people and remember that your closest friend was a stranger once." Others found companionship in the opposite sex but as one man said "I have a lady friend, but no hanky panky or smooching, just friends."

"Remember that your closest friend was a stranger once."

The next most popular response to coping with age related difficulties was being mentally tough and staying positive. More people elaborated on this than any other response naming it as the key component to all life experiences. It was virtually everyone's contention that when you lose the battle to stay positive the other battles will be lost one by one. This sentiment was expressed in comments like "you can't let it get you down," "don't wallow in your ageing," and "stay upbeat and focused on getting better because attitude is very important." Others elaborated on such feelings saying "stay mentally tough and keep fighting," "don't feel sorry for yourself," and "fight it; live life." One person said "I try to remind myself I'm better off than most." Others offered short bits of inspiration like "stay sharp," "stay hopeful," and "show determination."

"Stay mentally tough and keep fighting."

For some people inspiration came in the form of looking ahead to the future saying things like "plan ahead," "look forward to things," "think young," and "try not to worry." Still others focused on self improvement saying things like "I read a lot of self improvement books and smile a lot" and "I still seek advice and still have an open mind."

"I still seek advice and still have an open mind."

Keep in mind that many of the people making these statements were suffering from serious debilitation or even dying of disease and old age. That's why it is especially inspirational when they make comments like "look on the bright side, smile," "stay alive mentally and physically," and "stay positive. Keep your mind and body busy." One person had a simple formula for all life's difficulties saying "be positive, be friendly, and keep active." One particularly inspiring man encouraged everyone to "be enthusiastic about whatever you are doing. If you can't do something anymore then trade that enthusiasm for something else. Trade one thing like sailing for something else, like lawn bowling." This man was living proof that enthusiasm is transferable.

Three quotes capture the essence of what it means to stay positive in the face of adversity. One lady who had suffered terribly throughout her life said "I'm happy. I have lots of friends, a skip in my step and a twinkle in my eye. I'm a loyal friend." Another said "I wake up happy and make the best of every day." And perhaps the most inspirational comment was from a widow struggling with loneliness who said "work at it and stay positive. There is no magical formula to be happy. Choose to be happy."

"Work at it and stay positive. There is no magical formula to be happy. Choose to be happy."

Another key ingredient given for coping with age related difficulties is acceptance. Comments include "accept things as they are, accept your limitations," "live by your own standard," "take things as they come" and "try to make every day pleasant." Others live by a philosophy of acceptance saying things like "I resign myself to my situation," "I accept the fact that I'm getting old," and "I accept things as they are even though I don't like it." A similar sentiment was expressed by a person struggling with acceptance who said "I have a hard time accepting things but know I have to," and another who said "I cry sometimes but take it in stride." Another twist on acceptance came from a person who said "I'm trimming down my personal possessions," and another who said "I'm not envious of anyone."

"I have a hard time accepting things but know I have to."

Many people suffering themselves from age related difficulties found great relief in helping others. The philosophy was quite simple as people said things like "be good to other people," and "be a helper." One person said that it's important to "help people so I'm not just living for myself," and another said "I'm here to serve others and live life to the fullest with lots to do as a volunteer." Examples were many as people volunteered "driving seniors around," "delivering food, visiting the sick," "volunteering at a thrift store," "doing repairs for all the residents," "serving as secretary of a senior's group," "volunteering at the visually impaired place," "being a phone buddy," and "teaching classes." It seems that for many people the best way to deal with their own difficulties is helping others deal with some of theirs.

"I'm here to serve others and live life to the fullest."

Many people look to their faith and "spiritual stability" to help deal with age related difficulties and provide some contentment. For one person it is "leaning on the grace of God," and for another "looking forward to being with God." One lady who had lived a very difficult life and is struggling with illness said "my purpose is to do God's will and accept my place on earth as long as God wants me here."

"My purpose is to do God's will and accept my place on earth as long as God wants me here."

Medication is often used and abused by seniors to cope with age related illness but there was little direct mention of it in the interviews. Virtually every senior is on some kind of medication but most just made passing reference. A few people referred to "lots of medications" for various conditions, while another just said one word "Zoloft." For others it was self prescribed as one person said "happy hour," and another said "vodka is my medicine."

"Vodka is my medicine."

Health food and exercise seems like the lingo of young people but a surprising number of seniors spoke of working to stay healthy making comments like "eat properly," "take vitamins and health food," "go to exercise classes," and "workout at a gym." The most practical advice was to "do what the doctors say."

Other effective ways of dealing with age related difficulties are "maintaining a sense of humor," and "laughing lots." For others it is "keeping pace with the present," "being thankful to be here," and "being thankful for my blessings."

This chapter is full of optimism as well as pessimism, but the former wins out based on people's personal view of themselves and their place in the world. Given that, I wanted to get a sense of their view of the future of the world itself so I asked the question, Do you see much hope for the future of the world?

Unfortunately the optimism expressed in personal terms did not translate so well when looking at the current condition and future of the world. Twenty-nine percent of those asked said no they don't see much hope for the future of the world, thirty-six percent were fifty-fifty, some optimistic and some pessimistic but most unsure, and thirty-five percent said yes and were optimistic. The lone exception was the one person who said "I don't even think about it."

When asked about their view of the future of the world, most people answered fairly quickly, as though they had thought about it before. Beginning with the negative responses people made comments like "it's getting rougher all the time," "too many negative messages out there," "too much destruction," and "a big mess."

Others gave more specific responses and the reasons why they see little hope for the future with comments like "there are too many wars," "there are more have-nots than haves and war is our history," "once we got nuclear weapons it was the beginning of the end," and "the third world war is coming." For some it was war while others looked to politics, crime, society and religion making comments like "I feel very anxious about my great grandchildren and have no faith in world leaders," and "bad politicians." For many older people the world is not a safe place as reflected in comments like "things are getting worse, not safe," "problems seem to be escalating, more fanatics than ever before," and "the yellow race will rule the world."

"I feel very anxious about my great grandchildren and have no faith in world leaders."

Other problems for the world include population, pollution and disease as other negative responses include "not really, disease, wars, earthquakes," "population, disease, starvation," "pollution and religion." "We're killing our planet." Others pointed to "geological problems, earthquakes, Tsunamis, volcanoes, population," "weather," and "global warming. Young people have problems."

Many people pointed to uncertainty to support their pessimistic view of the future saying things like "I'm not sure about what's going to happen," "things are getting worse all the time," and "there's no common sense." Others added "things are moving too fast in the wrong direction," "things are getting worse rather than better," and "I'm really worried about the whole thing." One person said "I'm not sure but I think we've lived the best part of it," and "I wonder what the future holds for young people."

"I wonder what the future holds for young people."

Some people personalized their pessimism saying "I'm glad I lived when I did," "I'm glad I won't be here because I don't want to see what's coming," and "I'm glad I won't be here when the shit hits the fan with the environment." And one cynical person added "I don't give a damn anymore. I've only got about ten years left and I'm glad."

"I'm glad I lived when I did."

Not all negative responses were as pessimistic as some qualified their answer saying things like "unless miraculous changes take place," "it would take a miracle to teach people respect enough for us to survive," "this young generation doesn't have the respect anymore," and "we'd need to go back to basics and realize that we were all created equal and need to be treated equally." One pessimist shrugged his shoulders and said with resignation, "no, what will be will be."

Thirty-six percent of people responded fifty-fifty to whether they see hope for the future of the world, and answers in this category range from indifference, like "I don't speculate on the future but take it as it comes," to pessimistic then optimistic. The more negative fifty-fifty responses include many familiar comments like "things are moving too fast," "I don't see an end to wars and see more in the future," and "there will be a calamity of some sort that will change the world order." Others added "the white race will disappear, not sure what's going to happen," "atomic bombs," "multi-nationals creating problems, environmental issues," and "crime." The general outlook was there are "big problems ahead," "I'm thankful I won't be here for the coming trouble," and "I'm glad I won't be here."

"There will be a calamity of some sort that will change the world order."

Some people wanted to be hopeful saying things like "I'd like to but it's hard," and "there's a lot to worry about." In the fifty-fifty category I again heard comments about not wishing to be younger like "it's getting tougher," "I'm not sorry I'm seventy-three," "I'm glad I'm not growing up in this world right now," and "we lived in the best years in history." One person said with a quiet discomfort "I wonder if this is the beginning of the end."

"We lived in the best years in history."

Some struggled to be optimistic saying "the world cannot go on the way it is now," and "some things need to change." Politics and environment were key issues for some who said "the environment is in trouble so we need to fix it," "we need to look after resources, move to a one world government," and "the American government must change their view."

One person who wanted to be optimistic said "I worry about my grand children; we've got to get better or we'll fall apart." And looking to the bright side another person said "without hope there is no future," while another looked to divine assistance saying "only through faith in God, not through mankind."

Fortunately the negative comments did not carry the day as many comments were given about staying positive, being optimistic and working it out. The yes responses went from cautiously optimistic to almost Pollyanna enthusiasm. The cautious yes answers include qualifications like "but I wonder," "but it's scary," "it'll be tough," "we must learn something," and "we have problems that need to be addressed." One person had a 'skin of our teeth' approach saying "we will correct just in time." But others tried to be more practical in their assessment saying we have hope for the future "if they smarten up," "if we can keep the peace," and "if we all stick together we'll make it."

"If we all stick together we'll make it."

Others offered more views on areas getting improvement for a better world saying things like "governments are changing and aware of the environment," "there'll be another revolution," "if we can contain nuclear weapons," and "we'll carry on but the motor cars and pollution are killing us."

And finally the unqualified positive answers include "we'll work it out," "we will rebound," and "everyone is smarter now." It continued with comments like "there's so much more available," "always take the bright side," and "I try to think positive." It was refreshing to hear comments like "there is always hope," and "without hope you would have nothing."

"There is always hope."

There were some people who expressed faith in the younger generation saying "if I were twenty now I would just adapt to it," "the younger generation will work it out," "it will be a very different world ahead," and "I'm an optimist." Similar uplifting comments include "we can adapt to things, as we always have," "it will resolve itself," and "I'm very positive. We'll survive through adversity."

"The younger generation will work it out."

Not surprisingly some people look to their faith for optimism saying "God is there," "I think people are becoming more spiritual," "I pray for peace in the world, everyone should have their own God and faith," "we'll work it out, I believe in the end times," and "only in Christ."

"I pray for peace in the world."

Many older people's view of the future of the world was surprisingly pessimistic considering all they said about staying positive personally. It was a real disconnect for me as I thought it through, and I don't have a complete answer. Although their personal resolve remained strong I think that for many older people their resolve to fight for the future of the world has diminished. But I am convinced that given what many of them went through they would face the future now with the same resolve they did when they faced terrible circumstances like disease, the Depression and war. During this part of the interview I challenged several people with that and they agreed. In fact many of the stories they shared about the world they faced seem more difficult than the world we now face. I suppose it depends on one's perspective.

"We'll survive through adversity."

CHAPTER 10

DID YOUR LIFE MAKE A DIFFERENCE?

WE WOULD ALL LIKE to feel that we have made a difference in this world and left our mark in some way. In many ways this was the most emotional question as I asked people whose time is coming closer to the end "Does it matter that you lived? And do you feel that your life has made a difference in this world?" Some people admitted they had never really thought about it, much less been asked so directly. And most of the answers were qualified in some way as four percent said no, five percent said not sure and ninety-one percent said yes.

Those who said no offered self effacing comments like "I'm just a drop in the bucket," "I'm too minimal and unimportant," and "I hope so but don't really think so." Many responses alluded to accomplishing very little or feeling insignificant like "I haven't been aggressive enough in trying to get ahead," "I haven't done anything of significance, but I hope I've touched some people," and "I've done nothing outstanding." The most striking self description came from an eighty-five year old man who never married and said "I can't figure out why I was even born. I haven't accomplished anything. I'm very disappointed in myself."

"I can't figure out why I was even born. I haven't accomplished anything. I'm very disappointed in myself."

Those who gave a fifty-fifty response felt that their life mattered but understated its significance for reasons that ranged from exaggerated humility to disappointment in themselves. Comments include "I'm not sure but I hope so," "I could have done more," and "I'm not sure. I made a few people happy, my son and husband." One man who questioned his contribution to the world responded with no, then yes, then said "I worked hard, had kids but don't see my grandchildren much and my kids do their thing."

TOP TEN REASONS LIFE MADE A DIFFERENCE

▌ 1. Had children and raised family, grandchildren
▌ 2. Helped others
▌ 3. Worked hard
▌ 4. Was a good spouse
▌ 5. Positive influence / Touched lives
▌ 6. Lots of good friends / Good to people
▌ 7. Was a good parent
▌ 8. Was a good citizen, served my country / socially and politically active
▌ 9. Had good family relationships, mom, dad, siblings, etc
▌ 10. Teaching others

Ninety-one percent of those asked said yes they made a difference in this world and a surprising number of people named having children (and grandchildren) as their most significant contribution. Comments include "I brought five kids into the world," and "I had three children, gave them life, but nothing personally great." For many people bringing children in to the world and the extended family they began was the most significant, and sometimes only, difference they felt they had made.

Many people derive a great deal of life's meaning and significance from helping others which was the next most popular response and includes comments like "I'm a natural born care giver," "I helped people. I am a giver," and "I like people and try to help whenever and however I can."

"I like people and try to help whenever and however I can."

Nurses and other health care professionals made a career of helping others so were very assured about the difference they made saying things like "I looked after lots of people as a practical nurse," and "I helped lots of people as a nurse." A doctor said "I've helped people having been in the medical profession," and another health worker was proud to say "I worked at a good job caring for handicapped people." Some people were self described natural care givers, while others made a conscious and moral choice to enhance their own lives by helping to enhance the lives of others. "I'm a giver. I give of myself in many ways," "I helped lots of people by serving everyone all my life," and "I've helped lots of people and hope to be remembered as a caring person, wife, mother, and friend."

"I'm a giver. I give of myself in many ways."

The next most popular response involves hard work, and for those who said they worked hard it was primarily the personal satisfaction and sense of purpose derived from it that gave them a sense of meaning. But working hard and making a difference also included paying bills and doing what was expected of a responsible adult as reflected in comments like "I worked hard and ran a successful business," and "I was good to my staff, ran my business and supported my family." Recognizing their specific contribution others said "I worked hard and did valuable things in my job, stepped up when I needed to," and "I was a career RCMP member and did my best as a husband, father, and hard worker."

Being a good spouse was also stated by many as making a difference in their world but with little elaboration, perhaps because of the details given in the chapter on marriage. But general comments came from both husbands who worked hard and treated their wives with respect as well as wives who also worked hard and treated their husbands well.

Unlike the relatively few comments given about hard work and being a good spouse there were many comments about being a positive influence and touching the lives of others in some meaningful way. These ranged from the understated to profound including "I haven't done anything of significance but I hope I've touched some people," "I've spread lots of positive energy," and "I've spread some goodness in this world." Others added "I've been kind to lots of people," "I made a difference to the people I love," and "I've made a positive difference in many people's lives."

"I've made a positive difference in many people's lives."

Some people described their positive attitude as a lifestyle and were very aware of those they have influenced saying things like "I encouraged people to think positive," "I've been a good example to others," and "I have given confidence and happiness to others and been a positive influence with lots of ambition." One person was proud to say "a lot of people respected me," and another was happy to share how she has been affirmed saying "I've had people write me to tell me how I affected their life."

Displaying positive traits throughout their lives assured many people that they made a difference as reflected in comments like "I'm kind to everyone I meet," "I have no grudges and forgive people," and "I've been respectful to everyone. Every minute of my life has given me meaning." For one lady life is about "being happy and passing it on," then added, "I love life." Another said "I'm a positive person and pass that on to others. I'm always helping people. I didn't have riches but had happiness." Others were proud to say "I'm a very fair person, non-judgmental," and "I've been a peace maker. I was a good person."

"I didn't have riches but had happiness."

Spreading positive energy coincided with those who said that their life made a difference by having lots of good friends. Several comments include "I've had lots of good relationships," "I always loved people and got along well with them," and "I'm friendly and equal with people." One lady just smiled and said "my friends are my wealth."

"My friends are my wealth."

In previous responses having children and raising a family were very important to people and one of their primary contributions to the world, but there was also a related but separate response from those who felt that being a good parent was the way they made a difference. The difference they made was more than just having offspring for those who said "I raised my kids and did right by them," and "I supported my family and have good kids. They reflect me well." Further comments include "I was a good mom, a good example, always thinking of others," and "I was a good person and a good influence on my kids."

"I was a good person and a good influence on my kids."

Several mothers said with pride "I had seven kids that turned out great," "my daughters have education and good lives," and the most proud mom said "I had ten kids and looked after them so they're self sufficient and good people. My kids love me."

"My kids love me."

Many people felt that they contributed to their country through their children saying "I raised my kids to be good citizens," and "I did my best to be a good mom, and my greatest achievement is my kids." Then she added "my kids are good citizens." Another mom was proud to say "I raised three kids to be good citizens with Christian values."

Supporting their country was also very important to many people and the next most popular response came from those who said they made a difference by being good citizens, serving their country, and being politically and socially active. Many responses were general like "I contributed to society and the world," "I had lots of community involvement and social activities," and "I was part of groups working for society and organizations." Others offered similar comments like "I've been a helper, leader, and organizer," and "I've been very involved politically and socially and done lots of volunteer work. I did my part, without regrets."

Those who served in the armed forces were very proud of their contribution and every person that served in WWII named it as one of the ways they made a difference in the world by serving and defending their country.

Quite a few people were proud of their volunteer work and others mentioned their environmental work. One person was particularly proud of his contribution in Silva culture saying "I planted and grew lots of things that are growing. I planted hundreds of thousands of trees."

Good family relationships were recounted by many people as a significant contribution to the world. One person said "I was a good son," and another was proud to say "I was a good influence on my brothers and sisters, grandchildren, and family." One lady said "I made a difference to my children, my mother and my father," then added with a smile "my father was very proud of me."

As with health care professionals those in the teaching profession were very aware of their significant contribution. But also any people that served in a teaching capacity through their job or life circumstances were proud to have "contributed positive ideas and taught others."

Some people included their faith in the difference they made saying "I made a difference at the spiritual level. God had planned my life," and "I have a spiritual presence in this world. I have a purpose, helped lots of people, and listened a lot in Alanon and hospice." One person was proud of his pastoral work and another said "I've looked after lots of people and prayed for lots of people." One humble person said "I've been blessed by God and been a blessing to some others."

"I've been blessed by God and been a blessing to some others."

Supporting various charities and doing volunteer work continued to come up as people recounted their contributions "giving to charity, sponsoring children, "working with handicapped children," "donating time," and "helping various causes." One person said "I did lots of volunteer work and did some good somewhere along the way," and another summed it up saying "I've helped lots of people volunteering and really made an effort to improve the lives of others."

"I did lots of volunteer work and did some good somewhere along the way,"

Very much related to this were those who were proud of "working with kids and programs, lives we've touched," "sponsoring children, mentoring relationships, personal relationships," as well as raising foster kids.

For a number of people all the preceding contributions added up to "doing my part." One man said "I worked hard and did my part for society," and another said "I'm happy within myself, done my share for humanity. I did what I wanted and lived my life for my kids." Others were also confident with their contribution saying "I was a husband, father, and friend, and worked hard for many years. I did my part in this world," and "I did my duty to God and my country. I've helped lots of people and lived my faith."

"I worked hard and did my part for society,"

For others overcoming and doing their best was their most gratifying contribution. Comments include "I moved forward and overcame a lot, action oriented," "I straightened myself out and helped lots of people, helped lots of people in my work," and "I was an example to others about overcoming addiction." This was summed up by a person who said "I have done my best with the circumstances I was given," and another who added "I did the best I could each day and enjoyed my life."

Fun, laughter and entertainment were the way some people made a difference in the world as some said "I laughed a lot," "I've given love and laughs to lots of people," and "I could tell jokes." The more artistic types said things like "I've painted some pictures," "I played some good music and brought happiness to some people," and "I enjoyed myself as an entertainer and made people happy."

There were a few people who counted their love and concern for animals as a significant contribution to the world saying "I cared for lots of animals, rescued lots," and "I enjoy living, helped lots of people in my job as a male nurse, and I was good to animals."

One person said he made a difference "only in that I was here." There were many such comments like "I worked hard and helped people but haven't done much of anything," and "Yes, but only in the last few years." One lady who had been terribly abused and mistreated most of her life emerged from her bitterness long enough to say that her contribution to the world was "I could dance."

A few responses were self questioning or uncertain like "I'm not sure what will be said in my eulogy," "we're all here for some reason," and "in the old days I worked hard and raised kids. I made a difference for me." One person just said of the difference he made "the proof will only be known in the future," and perhaps the most indifferent answer about making a difference in the world was "yes, but I don't think much about it. I'm just living my life." Most people were happy to reflect on their contribution to the world, especially after being asked directly. It was a defining moment for some.

CHAPTER 11

CONCLUSION

AFTER THE INTERVIEW was complete I had a column for further comments and sometimes wrote a note to myself as an afterthought or impression. Some people were very impressive in the way they expressed themselves and there were a few interviews that left me shaking my head at the simple profundity lived out before me. After one such interview I wrote "this was an excellent interview with a very impressive, intelligent and articulate lady." Similar comments include "this was an inspirational eighty-nine year old, well spoken, clear headed, engaging, active and still living on his own," and "this person typifies a generation that worked hard, accepted struggle and didn't feel the world owed him anything. He worked very hard with little complaint and was thankful for the opportunity."

There were also several couples who had a deep impact on me in the way they understood each other and their life together. Some were very progressive for their generation and were equally empowered, something the wife especially appreciated. One such interview caused me to write "this was a very well adjusted and content couple, best I have interviewed, who have lived a happy and fulfilled life together."

There were also some interviews that were not so inspiring. Some people seemed medicated or distracted by illness while others acted doomed and interpreted the world through that lense. Others lived in dismal conditions like a smelly old apartment with old and broken furniture or a hospital-type shared room in which they were not happy. For many it affected their state of mind knowing they didn't have the ability to change their living environment and that it would remain that way until death. After one such interview I wrote "there was tremendous pain in this person. She was very guarded about revealing painful things of the past and cried much of the time during the interview."

Others lived in an unhappy relationship and made that clear. When asked if they were happily married one couple looked at each other and both said "not really." We then discussed marital issues and the nature of their unhappiness for well over an hour. There were many such moments during the interviews when the conversation took on a counseling tone as we discussed issues from the past or present. For many people the questions I asked provided an opportunity to speak with someone about things that had been on their mind, sometimes for many years, but had not been asked about so directly. Having trained as a counselor I appreciated the opportunity to have such discussions and was happy to give of my time in the context of asking for theirs.

Along with my thoughts and impressions, I sometimes invited an afterthought or final word from the person being interviewed asking if there is anything else they would like to say or any final advice they would like to pass on to the younger generation. Most declined but some offered further comments.

Amongst the final comments were the usual disappointments with the younger generation such as "young people have had things too easy," "kids now don't know what it's like to do without," and "people now seem softer. We were harder and went through the Depression and the War." The older ways continued on the minds of many of those who lived through it saying "during the Depression many people helped each other," and "we used to do things that were simpler and enjoyed them very much."

"People now seem softer. We were harder and went through the depression and the war."

There were many more bits of advice about being positive and setting one's course with familiar admonitions like "you have to take responsibility and build your own life," "be true to yourself, set your own course in life," and "there's no such thing as a mistake, only experience. Be grateful and keep a positive outlook." One person profoundly said "the most important thing in life is success, and success is measured by happiness. Your mind is like the steering wheel on the car, you have to hold it tight or it gets away on you."

"The most important thing in life is success, and success is measured by happiness."

Many people offered more specific advice like "help in the fight against drugs," "always have money and you can enjoy life a lot more," and "live in the moment, focused, attentive." Some shared things they had learned along the way like "in business and in life assess strengths, weaknesses, opportunities, and threats (SWOTs)," and "remember the law of unintended consequences." Another person said he was enlightened by *The Four Agreements* by Don Miguel Ruiz, and another offered the timeless reminder "humor is the most important factor in life."

"Live in the moment, focused, attentive."

There were many last bits of advice on relationships and treatment of others. For child rearing there was advice like "in raising kids give them roots and wings," while more general bits of advice include "live to affect others in a positive way," "do nice things for people because you never know the seeds you plant," and "seek peace and lots of hugs." One person who believed in reincarnation said "I'm working to be better so when I come back I can reach a higher level."

"Live to affect others in a positive way."

There were a few comments that emerged after the interview that made me glad I asked for an afterthought. One person said "for a bad person Might is Right, but for a good person Right is Might," and "I talked to a six year old dying of cancer and it made me realize I don't have problems. He changed my life. Do things without expecting recognition." And some lasting words of wisdom from two people include "contentment means I'm not going after things I can't possibly have," and perhaps the best comment of all "I'm not good looking, I'm not rich, and I'll never be president, but I can look in the mirror and like myself."

"I'm not good looking, I'm not rich, and I'll never be president, but I can look in the mirror and like myself."

Doing over three hundred interviews was a long and often difficult process so I really appreciate those who understood my task and helped me complete it. Without them I might have been too discouraged to finish. Thanks to those who participated in the interviews but thanks also to those who didn't because both taught me a great deal. I was sometimes confused and always disappointed by those who ran in the other direction at the thought of talking about their lives, those who felt too vulnerable to be exposed in such a way or seemed irritated that someone would ask. Some people remain guarded and closed for their entire life and miss many opportunities as a result, not the least of which the opportunity to pass on some of their wisdom. I was also disappointed with some senior's groups, Veteran's clubs and care homes who said their people didn't want to be bothered by interviews. I interviewed many of them through the side door from personal references and it turns out they appreciated the opportunity.

For me, one of the best parts of this experience was learning things that I didn't expect to, not the least of which is that old people are in many ways young people. They are me, and you, and us. As I began the interviewing process I learned to see the young person in the eyes of the older person as they talked of their childhood. I quickly realized that childhood experiences stay with us for a lifetime as I sat with people over eighty years old who spoke vividly of childhood experiences, both good and bad, as though they happened yesterday. This confirmed for me that we truly are a collection of our experiences and that many older people really are younger people living in old bodies.

I can't overstate how profoundly so many people touched my life. I interviewed some people I can't remember but I met many people I will never forget, especially those who went through untold misery and still found a way to be happy. I thank them for their inspiration and will do my best to pass it on. We can all learn a great deal from what they went through and how they survived. For the most part they are a generation of people that stepped up to their challenges and survived, even thrived.

I end with an attempt to sum up what I learned from them: **A vibrant spirit shines youthful from an ageing body, hard work builds character that can't be achieved in any other way, and happiness, meaning and contentment have more to do with attitude than circumstance.**

QUESTIONAIRE

DATE OF INTERVIEW:_____

PREAMBLE. This interview is conducted as part of the research I'm doing for a study. Only your first name is required, and the information you provide will not be related explicitly to you. It will only be referred to as part of the findings. I will ask you a series of questions that I hope you will answer frankly and honestly. If you are not comfortable answering a particular question, simply say you'd prefer not to answer and we'll move on to the next question. My goal is not to pry into your life or ask overly personal questions. Rather, my goal is to gain insights and wisdom from your life and experience.

NAME	GENDER	AGE	P.O.B.

ETHNICITY	
LEVEL OF EDUCATION	
TIMES MARRIED	
CURRENT STATUS	
NUMBER OF CHILDREN	

■ What was (is) your primary Occupation (s)?_____
_____
_____

■ Did you enjoy your work?_____
_____
_____

■ What did you like most about your work?_____
_____
_____

■ What did you like least about your work?_____
_____
_____

■ Did you move a lot or stay mostly in one place?_____
_____
_____

■ Did (Do) you own a home or did you prefer to rent?_____
_____
_____

■ Did you take lots of holidays? Where?_____
_____
_____

■ Were you involved in any clubs, organizations or charity work? If so, which ones?_____
_____
_____

■ Did you practice a religion or go to church? If Yes, What religion / denomination?_____

_____

_____

■ What is the hardest thing you've ever had to deal with?_____

_____

_____

■ Would you say you have had a happy life?_____

_____

_____

■ Why? What are the reasons you were happy / sad?_____

_____

_____

■ Were you (or are you) "happily" married? Yes / no? What made it happy / unhappy?_____

_____

_____

■ What was the biggest mistake you ever made?_____

_____

_____

■ As you think back over your life, what are your 3 biggest regrets?

    1._____

     _____

    2._____

     _____

3._____
_____

■ If you could live your life over again what are three things you would change?

1._____
_____

2._____
_____

3._____
_____

■ If you were to give a younger person three pieces of advice what would they be?

1._____
_____

2._____
_____

3._____
_____

■ Are you more patient now you're older, or less patient?_____
_____
_____

■ Are you a grumpy older or happy person? Why?_____
_____
_____

■ How do you think young people see you? _____

_____

_____

■ How would you like young people to see you? _____

_____

_____

■ Do you remember your youth often? _____

_____

_____

■ Would you say you live in the past? _____

_____

_____

■ Do you still feel young at heart? _____

_____

_____

■ What's the best part of growing old? _____

_____

_____

■ What's the worst part of growing old? _____

_____

_____

■ How do you minimize the worst parts of growing old? _____

_____

_____

■ Do you own a computer? _____

_____

■ Are you on line? _____

_____

_____

■ Do you own a cell phone? _____

_____

_____

■ Do you see much hope for the future of the world? _____

_____

_____

■ Do you feel like your life has made a difference in this world? _____

_____

_____

■ In what ways? _____

_____

_____

I, the above named, have participated in this questionnaire of my own free will and hereby authorize the interviewer to use my statements anonymously as part of a published work.

DATE:

SIGNATURE_____

.

■ Further Comments:_____

_____

TOP TEN LISTS

TOP TEN DISLIKES ABOUT WORK

1. Long hours, shifts
2. Bosses, management, union
3. Very hard work, pressure, responsibility
4. Some co-workers
5. Low pay
6. Some customers
7. Being away from home
8. Getting up early
9. Commuting
10. Feeling like a number

TOP TEN LIKES ABOUT WORK

1. Enjoy People, customers, coworkers, etc.
2. Helping others
3. Challenging, hard work
4. Making money and paying bills
5. Interesting
6. Freedom, no desk, own boss
7. Variety
8. Sense of accomplishment
9. Had a natural ability for it
10. Learning things

TOP TEN REASONS FOR A HAPPY LIFE

1. Happy marriage
2. Kids and grandkids
3. Family and friends
4. Good Job and satisfying work
5. Just a naturally happy person
6. Good parents and happy childhood
7. Lucky
8. God / Faith / Church
9. Freedom to pursue life
10. Love people

TOP TEN REGRETS

1. Not enough education.
2. Not pursuing the job I really wanted.
3. Not pursuing arts more, music, dance, acting, art.
4. Not "going for it." Procrastination, missed opportunities.
5. Not being a better parent or family person
6. Not having enough money.
7. Not travelling more.
8. Getting married too young or to the wrong person.
9. Not being wiser when younger.
10. Not having a child or more children.

TOP TEN QUESTIONS TO ASK FOR JOB SATISFACTION.

1. Do you enjoy people, coworkers, bosses, customers, associates?
2. Do you have a sense that you're helping others in your work?
3. Do you find your work challenging in some way?
4. Do you feel satisfaction that you're making money and paying bills?
5. Do you find your work interesting in some way?
6. Do you have a sense of freedom in your job, physical, mental or creative?
7. Is there some variety to your work?
8. Do you feel a sense of accomplishment in your work?
9. Do you have a natural ability for what you're doing?
10. Are you learning things at your work?

TOP TEN HARDEST THINGS YOU'VE EVER HAD TO DEAL WITH

1. Death of a spouse, child, family, friends.
2. Seeing loved ones sick or injured
3. Loss of health, cancer, disease, debilitation
4. Financial loss of job or investment
5. Divorce
6. Raising kids, supporting family.
7. Family drug and alcohol problems
8. WWII, war
9. Childhood trauma, Family breakup.
10. Farm work, hard work / The Great Depression

TOP TEN PIECES OF ADVICE

1. Get an education
2. Think things through, have a plan, set goals
3. Get some kind of career, vocation, trade or training.
4. Find the right mate
5. Have good morals, honest, respectful, good character
6. Find out what you enjoy and pursue it
7. Avoid debt and live within your means
8. Have a positive attitude and do the best you can in everything you do
9. Know yourself, establish yourself, and be your own person
10. Work Hard

TOP TEN REASONS GIVEN FOR LONG AND HAPPY MARRIAGE

1. Compatibility
2. Loving each other / caring / considerate
3. Being friends / having fun / doing stuff together
4. Working together to build a life
5. Seeing your partner as a good person
6. Working at it to get along / Communication
7. One or both being laid back or happy go lucky
8. Kids / family / home
9. Trust / Mutual respect
10. Faith

TOP TEN ANSWERS TO THE BEST PART OF GROWING OLD

1. Freedom, more time to do what I want, social events, travel, etc.
2. Still relatively healthy and active
3. Content and enjoying my life.
4. Less pressure, responsibility, worry, anxiety and concern.
5. Financial Stability / Pension
6. No Best Part
7. Doing Lots, Staying Busy, Hobbies
8. Retirement, not having to work
9. Family, kids, grandkids
10. Wiser, learned a lot

TOP TEN ANSWERS TO THE WORST PART OF GROWING OLD

1. Aches and Pains, Physical limitations, Lack of energy
2. Being inactive, Can't get out and do as much like travel and activities
3. Nothing, No worst part
4. Serious Illness, cancer, stroke, etc.
5. Loss of Family and Friends
6. Loneliness and depression
7. Loss of Independence, Being a Burden, Needing Care
8. Looking ahead to Illness and Death
9. Getting old and wanting to be younger
10. Loss of memory and brain functioning

TOP TEN ANSWERS TO, "HOW DO YOU MINIMIZE THE WORST PARTS OF GROWING OLD?"

1. Stay Busy / hobbies / social activities, etc
2. Family and friends
3. Stay Positive and mentally tough.
4. Acceptance, Take Life as it Comes
5. Help others, Volunteer
6. Faith / Church / Prayer
7. Medication to Control things
8. Try to Stay Healthy
9. Laughing / Sense of Humor
10. Live in the Present and BE Thankful

TOP TEN REASONS LIFE MADE A DIFFERENCE

1. Had children and raised family, grandchildren
2. Helped others
3. Worked hard
4. Was a good spouse
5. Positive influence / Touched lives
6. Lots of good friends / Good to people
7. Was a good parent
8. Was a good citizen, served my country / socially and politically active
9. Had good family relationships, mom, dad, siblings, etc.
10. Teaching others

ISBN 142518625-4

9 781425 186258